THE
PRIMROSE PATH

Sonia Harrison Jones

THE
PRIMROSE PATH

EP

Erser & Pond

Cover design by Benjamin Beaumont

Printed in the U.S.A. by Erser & Pond Publishers, Ltd.

1096 Queen St., Suite 225, Halifax, N.S., Canada B3H 2R9

Library and Archives Canada Cataloguing in Publication

Jones, Sonia
    The primrose path / Sonia Jones.

Includes index.
ISBN 978-0-9781761-4-3

    1. Pond, Marion Belle. 2. Pond, Percy--Family. 3. Jones, Sonia--Family. 4. Pond family. 5. Harrison family.
6. Connecticut--Biography.

I. Title.

F101.3.H37J65 2008   974.6'0430922   C2008-902197-5

Second Edition

This book is dedicated to
my mother,
Heather Harrison
(née Marion Belle Pond);
with gratitude and love.

Heather Harrison, London, England, 1929

PHOTOGRAPHS OF
THE POND FAMILY

Percy Pond's father and mother, Louis Jaszynsky and Marion Blanchard, were married in San Francisco in 1870, when Louis was 27. He died ten years later, when Percy was eight years old. In 1883 his widow married a Mr. E. S. Pond, who adopted young Percy and gave him his name.

Harriet Hall Pond, ca 1908

Harriet Hall Pond and
Marion Belle Pond, 1909

Percy Pond and his son, Edwin Pond, ca 1904.

Photo by Dorothy Wilding

Marion Belle Pond, shortly after her marriage to Kay Harrison on February 5th, 1927

FAMILY PORTRAITS BY STELLA MARKS
(the author's aunt)

Photo by Bertram Follet

Stella Marks at work on H.R.H. Prince Charles, 1952

Oil painting: Kay Harrison, 1946

Oil painting in miniature
of Sonia Harrison, 1940

Portrait of Sonia Harrison, 1948

Portrait of Nigel Harrison, 1944

PHOTOGRAPHS OF THE HARRISON FAMILY

Mrs. Edwin Percy Pond
1873-1957

Kay Harrison
1895-1962

Mrs. Kay Harrison
1904-1995

Photo by Sonia Jones

Sheila Harrison
1930-

Craig Harrison
1933-

Gordon Jones
1930-

Sonia Harrison
(Later Mrs. Gordon Jones)
1938-

Wilda Harrison
(Later Mrs. John Gallagher)
1940-

Nigel Harrison
1941-

Heather Harrison (Jr.)
(Later Mrs. Scott Hurley)
1946-

PROLOGUE

Between the years of 1955 and 1966, my mother wrote me a ream of letters carefully inscribed in dark blue ink on onion skin paper. The letters overflowed with love, encouragement, sympathy, wisdom, humor, and some excellent pieces of motherly advice. I was in my teens and twenties back then, and I could only see the "advice" parts of her letters, which I didn't want to know anything about. I recall (with horror) how disappointed I used to be when I received a letter from my mother instead of a *billet doux* from the boyfriend of the moment. I didn't want her advice. I knew everything already. I felt her opinions were old-fashioned and totally irrelevant to the bright, modern new world I lived in.

But I never threw her letters out. They were from my mom, after all, and she had taken much time and effort to write those pages about how a well-brought-up young lady should behave with a gentleman if she wanted him to find her interesting. Sometimes her words of advice would alight on the topic of human nature in general, using as examples the personalities in her immediate orbit such as her father, Percy Pond the photographer; or her mother, Hattie Hall the belle of the ball; or her brother, Edwin Pond, the brat who sometimes deigned to be nice to her. I used to love reading about Edwin, for like most people my age, I found deviltry far more amusing and exciting than guidance on how to develop good manners and good listening skills.

Then my mother died, after a long and difficult struggle with Alzheimer's disease. Suddenly I missed her. I missed her with all my heart. I yearned for her to write me letters, to tell me how to understand people, to describe to me all over again what it was like to be born and brought up in Alaska at the turn of the century.

I wanted to know what she had enjoyed about her friends at the University of California at Berkeley, and what she recalled about her years in Tokyo in the late 1920s, and how she had learned to deal with a mercurial, unpredictable, creative, witty, passionate, and daunting man like my father. Why had I been too busy to spend more time with her?

I dug out her letters again and began to read them at my desk in our condo in Halifax, Nova Scotia. Within minutes I was starting to cry, putting the pen-and-ink letters at risk of being lost forever. When I saw how loving she was in those letters, I could only remember the many times I had treated her badly. I would complain that she didn't understand my generation, and she responded with patience. I'd be irritated with her for not remembering something, and she would be gracious enough to apologize. I would accuse her unfairly of making poor decisions, and she'd respond kindly.

It was unconditional love, and I didn't recognize it. She was the one who taught me about the love of the mother who was prepared to give her baby to the prostitute rather than let Solomon cut him in half. It was she who taught me about the love of the father for the prodigal son. It was my mother who modeled the love of God for his children. And for this I shall always be grateful.

This book is not meant to be a biography or an academic treatise. It is a memoir of my maternal family, in which I do my best to capture the spirit of the various personalities. This involves a little imagination and a touch of creativity, as well as some assumptions about the nature of conversations that took place in my absence or before I was born. But a book without dialogue would be dull indeed, especially when it involves a group of vibrant, distinctive individuals. I beg the forgiveness of anyone who feels misrepresented.

The names of some of the non-family members have been changed to protect their privacy. A few details of their lives have also been altered for the same reason.

ACKNOWLEDGMENTS

I am grateful to Kay Shelton, the Director of the Alaska State Library in Juneau, and to James Simard, Gladi Kulp, and Sandra Johnston (also of the Alaska State Library) for their help in locating photos and information about Percy Pond. I am also deeply grateful to my grandfather's friend, George Jorgenson, for rescuing close to 4,700 glass plate and nitrate film negatives after *Winter and Pond* was dissolved. I am beholden to his son, William Jorgenson, for seeing to it that the Alaska State Library was able to make the work of Winter and Pond available to the general public.

I am indebted to Victoria Wyatt for her book, *Images from the Inside Passage: An Alaskan Portrait by Winter & Pond,* in which she reprints photographs by my grandfather and his talented partner, Lloyd Winter. This is a superb work of scholarship and has been of great value to anthropologists, historians, photographers and to the general public as well.

I am grateful to Robert DeArmond for his condensed version of Wendy Calmensen's "Winter and Pond: Pioneer Photographers in Alaska, 1893-1943" (Master's thesis, San Francisco State College, 1979) that appeared in the Winter, 1982 edition of *The Alaska Journal.* I highly recommend it to those seeking information about Alaska's frontier days.

Finally, I owe much of my knowledge of the maternal side of my family to the many vivid and entertaining stories related to me by my grandmother, Harriet Hall Pond, and by my mother, Heather Harrison (née Marion Belle Pond). I also made liberal reference to their correspondence with me over the years. Please see the Appendix at the end of this book for samples of their hand-written letters.

CHAPTER ONE

My mother suffered from a rather unusual form of Alzheimer's disease, for she began living her life in reverse. Her most recent memories made the least impact on her, so they didn't remain with her for very long. Her oldest childhood memories were the most vivid ones, so they lingered to the end. She had a rather befuddled idea of the present, a fairly clear picture of her childbearing years, and quite a sound memory of her engagement and marriage. But she recalled her early childhood in such lucid detail that eventually it became the only reality she knew.

I must admit that it took me a while to put two and two together. I first began to notice her memory lapses when she'd forget to come and get us from school. If I was lucky I'd have a nickel and I'd go call her from the payphone in the dining hall. She'd arrive about fifteen minutes later, looking frazzled and apologetic, and I'd slam the car door to show her how aggravating it was for us to always be the last ones to leave the school grounds. I figured that if I showed my dissatisfaction emphatically enough, she'd eventually get the hint and make the effort to pick us up on time.

I saw the problem only from my own point of view, of course. I thought she didn't care enough about us to bother to get us on time, so I'd be cranky and resentful. Maybe if my mother had been perfectly honest with us and confessed that her memory was getting shaky and that she needed some help with the problem, I might have understood a little better what was going on. But on the other hand, maybe I wouldn't have had the maturity back then to put myself in her place. I was the center of my own little world, and all that mattered to me was that I resented having a mother who couldn't seem to remember me from one minute to the next. I wanted to be the center of her world. I wanted her to be so impatient to see me that she'd be the very *first* mom to arrive at the school. I'm embarrassed now to think back on how self-centered I was in those days.

Honesty hurts at any age, so my mom probably couldn't bring herself to confess that her memory was failing. She always came up with some excuse about how she had tried to get out of the house on time but someone had called her on the telephone, or someone had knocked on the door, or Josy had dropped a casserole on the kitchen floor, or she had been held up at the hairdresser's.

"Did he have a gun?" Nigel would ask.

"What?" my mother would say, looking blank.

"The crook that held you up at the hairdresser's. Did he have a gun?"

She would look relieved then, knowing that Nigel could always be counted upon to add a little humor to the situation, which was his way of telling her she was forgiven. I would glare at him, trying to let him know with a meaningful look that he was forgiving her much too quickly. It would be better to glower for a little while longer so she'd realize how upset we were about being abandoned at school like waifs at an orphanage.

Wilda was no help at all. She didn't even care that Mom was forever late. It was a matter of complete indifference to her that she was lateness personified. She was the epitome of lateness. Lateness in the flesh. Lateness on two legs that never took her anywhere on time. I would cross my arms and try to scowl enough for the three of us. Wilda would just shrug and look out the window, oblivious to the way Mom would brake for every blowing leaf as though it were going to cause a fatal accident.

Honesty. Would it have helped if she *had* told us she'd forgotten us rather than making up excuses for being late? I suppose it wouldn't have been good enough for me, for I still probably would have suspected that I wasn't worthy of being remembered. But if a physician had told me that she had a disease called early onset Alzheimer's, and that her constant forgetfulness had nothing at all to do with her not loving me enough to remember me, then this would have made all the difference in the world. But nobody paid much attention to what was generally referred to as "senility" in those days, even though "senile" would have seemed like a strange way to describe my 50-year-old mother. I'm sure she would have been mortified by such a diagnosis anyway, and she would have written the doctor off as a died-in-the-wool quack.

The truth is I'm not very sure about the accuracy of the "early onset" part of her condition (that term was not yet used in those days). In fact, I'm not even certain she *had* a disease back in those early years. Her memory lapses may have been due almost entirely to the stress caused by the general chaos in her life. Not only did she have six unruly children who were always pulling in different directions, but my widowed grandmother lived on the ground floor of our sprawling house, where she could remind my mother in a loud, judgmental voice that children were supposed to be seen and not heard. Granted, Mom did have Josy to do the cooking and cleaning, but Josy was the kind of person who needed excitement in her life, and she liked to make mischief when things were going too smoothly. Add to that mixture three turtles and a cat that was secretly responsible for the constantly dwindling number of goldfish in the pool under the fountain in the breakfast room, and you get the picture.

All this became supremely understandable to me when I was old enough to have accumulated some equally stressful experiences in my own life. By the time I was forty I was chairing a university department, running a yogurt business, caring for two small children, and commuting back and forth to work for two-and-half hours a day. Although my mother's life was not an exact duplicate of mine, I was busy enough to know that stress can play havoc with the memory. When I forgot an appointment or a student's name, I would go into a tailspin. *Good grief! Is this early onset Alzheimer's?*

It was around then that I experienced the painful effect that Alzheimer's disease can have on other family members. It was a Saturday morning in June. It was such a gorgeous day that I decided to phone my mother, thinking how much she would have enjoyed our beautiful, peaceful farm in Nova Scotia, with brown cows grazing on the green, green grass.

"Hi, Mom! How are you doing?"

"Fine, thank you. How are you?" she answered politely.

Oops. Either she was mad at me for some reason, or she was being held at gunpoint and was being forced to pretend that everything was just fine.

"Mom? What's the matter?"

There was a short pause.

"Why, nothing at all. I'm very well, thank you."

I struggled to remember what I might have done to make her angry. Had I let too much time go by between calls? It wasn't like her, though, to be sarcastically pleasant when she was angry. She wasn't the martyr type. I decided to use the direct approach rather than beat around the bush.

"Are you mad at me, Mom?"

"Why no, of course not. I just... Well, I'm just trying to think why you're calling me *Mom*."

So that was it. She was becoming hard of hearing. She didn't recognize my voice.

"It's me, Sonia!" I said, raising my voice so she could hear me better. "I'm your daughter, Sonia."

Another pause.

"I see," she said vaguely. "Well, that name isn't familiar to me, I'm afraid."

I felt my face flush with fear and shock.

"Mom? Did you fall down? Did you hurt your head? Are you sure you're all right?"

"I'm very well, thank you," she said once again.

"Are you sure you don't know the name *Sonia?*"

She paused to think for a while.

"No, I'm sorry, but I don't know that name," she said. "Perhaps you have the wrong number," she added helpfully.

"What about *Fay?* Do you remember your friend, Fay?"

"Why yes," she said, brightly. "Fay was my best friend when I was growing up in Juneau, Alaska. We used to play with each other all the time. She was Uncle Bart's little girl, and Big Fay was her mother."

"Exactly! That's right, Mom," I said, feeling relieved. "Well, *Fay* is my middle name. You named me after your friend, Fay Thane."

Another pause.

"How did you say you got that name? Did you know Fay? Did you know Uncle Bart? Are you from Juneau?"

"No, Mom. I've never been to Alaska."

How could this have happened so quickly? It hadn't been *that* long since I last called her. It was as though she had died, but was still talking to me on the phone. It was her voice, and I loved hearing her voice, but she wasn't there anymore. I never expected her to disappear that way. She was gone, but I could still hear her voice.

"You've never been to Alaska?" Mom said, sounding puzzled. "Then how do you know Fay? The Thane family eventually moved to Niles. Did you meet her in Niles?"

"No, I've never been to Niles."

"It's in Alameda County, in California."

"I know. You've told me a lot about Niles."

"When did I tell you about Niles?"

"All my life, Mom. You used to tell me stories about Niles, and Juneau, and San Francisco, and Uncle Bart, and your brother Edwin, and your husband Kay, and your father, Percy Pond, alias Primrose, and your mother, Hattie Hall…"

"Yes, my mother's name is Hattie Hall. But I should go now, as I'm expecting Kay to come home soon. I'd like to put on my make-up now so I can look nice for him when he comes through the doorway. It was kind of you to telephone me. I very much enjoyed our conversation. I hope you'll call on us soon. My husband will be very pleased to meet you."

My mother had lost her memory, but she hadn't lost her good manners. How strange that good manners can be more a part of oneself than the memory of one's own children.

"I forgot to ask you, where do you live?"

"We're staying at Grosvenor House."

"In London?"

"Why, yes. In London, of course."

I could tell by her tone of voice that she thought it was peculiar that I had to check to be sure that Grosvenor House was in London. She probably thought I was in London too, and that I was making a local call. Long distance calls were relatively rare back in the days when she lived at Grosvenor House. They always involved overseas operators who made the call sound important by asking the receiver to hold the line for an incoming call from the United States, or wherever it happened to be coming from.

"What's the address?" I asked.

"It's on Park Lane, in Mayfair. Near Hyde Park. You can't miss it."

"Is there a number?"

"A telephone number?"

"No, I mean a street number."

"I'm afraid I can't remember the street number. But you needn't worry. Every taxi driver knows just where it is."

"Thank you so much for the kind invitation. I'll be sure to call on you one day soon. Goodbye for now."

"Goodbye. Thank you for your telephone call."

I sat back in my chair, needing a little time to recuperate. My brain was going a mile a minute. If my mom believed she was living in Grosvenor House, that meant she thought it was 1929. She had married my dad on February 5th, 1927, when she was 22 years old and a recent graduate from the University of California at Berkeley. They'd moved directly to Japan, where they'd lived for two years while my dad started a new branch of his business in Tokyo. Once the branch office was up and running, they'd moved to London and stayed at Grosvenor House for a few months while they looked for a permanent residence. They finally bought a townhouse at 49 Charles Street, just off Berkeley Square. But if Mom told me on the phone that she was still at Grosvenor House, it meant that she didn't have any children yet. No wonder she thought it was weird that I was calling her *Mom*. She might have even thought it was a bit strange that I was saying *Mom* instead of *Mummy*, which is what we called her when we were children growing up in London. We had switched over to *Mom* when we'd moved to the U.S. so we'd be more like everyone else. Besides, by that time we knew enough about Egypt to feel turned off by the crypt-like connotations.

I decided to call my sister Sheila and find out what was going on. Sheila lived with Mom and cared for her, so she'd be able to give me the real scoop, after I interpreted what she had to say. Sheila was very intelligent, but she had her own peculiar way of seeing things. She was the first child, born on November 19th, 1930, shortly after my parents moved to 49 Charles Street. My mother always thought there was something a bit wrong, but since she was her first baby, she laid it down to her own ignorance. Still, she thought it was unusual that Sheila was so easily startled and so wary of strangers. She didn't seem to like being held in anyone's arms, and she seemed frightened of things that nobody else would even notice. Eventually she had been diagnosed with "childhood schizophrenia," which was later called "autism."

She lived very much in her own world, but she enjoyed our company even so. This was surprising, since by nature she was an enemy of chaos, and the five of us provided her with more than enough to satisfy an army. So to balance the turmoil of her daily life she pursued activities that gave her the opportunity of contemplating perfect order and harmony. She developed an interest in needlework of all kinds, such as knitting, tatting, crocheting, and cross-stitching. Later, when they failed to be intricate enough to fulfill her insatiable need for perfection, she began weaving the most extraordinary bedspreads and tablecloths. There were never any mistakes in anything she did, for she would see to it that they were eliminated at once. There was no room in her mind for error, so this meant she had to completely avoid the performing arts. She had made an effort to learn to play the piano, but every time she made a mistake she would have to start all over again right from the beginning. My mother eventually couldn't take it anymore, so Sheila was quietly encouraged to pursue the art of weaving instead.

It was time, now, for me to give her a call and find out what was happening with Mom.

"Hi, Sheila," I said, when she answered the phone. "It's me, Sonia."

"Oh, hello Sonia," she replied, in her laconic voice.

"So what's going on with Mom? I called her today, and she didn't know who I was."

"She's fine," Sheila said. "She made shirred eggs this morning for breakfast."

"Shirred eggs? I haven't had those in years!"

"Well, she over-baked them, I'm afraid. But I didn't say anything. I didn't want to offend her, so I ate them anyway."

"That was very kind of you. You did the right thing."

"Oh, thank you!" she said, with unfeigned pleasure.

My mother had spent many years teaching Sheila how other people felt and how to treat them "nicely," so she was always very pleased to be told that she had succeeded.

"Sheila, does Mom know who you are?"

"Yes, she does. She believes I'm her mother."

"Her *mother*? What does she think when she looks in the mirror, then?"

"She sees her reflection in it."

"Yes, but doesn't she see she's much older than you are? How can she imagine that you're *her* mother?"

"It's because I do things for her, like make the toast and fill her hot water bottle, and things like that."

"Good for you! What would she do without you?"

"She'd skip the toast, and her feet would be cold."

"Does she ever wonder where Dad is?"

"She says he's away on business."

"Does she miss him?"

"I don't know. She doesn't tell me whether she misses him or not. She talks about him a lot, though. She makes plans. She thinks about all the things she'll do for him when he comes home. She says she wants to be the perfect wife. Sometimes I wish *I* had a husband to plan things for."

"What would you do if you had one?"

"I'd knit him argyle socks and wool sweaters so he'd be warm. And we'd have children and go for long walks. I'd teach them all the bird calls and the names of the flowers."

She would, too. There wasn't a bird or a flower in the State of Connecticut that Sheila didn't know.

"Do you think Mom is happy, Sheila?"

"Yes, I think she is. She likes to play make-believe and pretend that Daddy's still alive. It's a game she plays. She doesn't know it, but I play those games, too. I've done that all my life. I think she's decided that it's fun to play make-believe when you're feeling sort of bored with everyday life. That way you can make things turn out the way you want them to."

I heard her give a little sigh of contentment.

"Don't tell anybody, okay?" she added.

"Why not? There's nothing wrong with what you're doing. Everybody likes to daydream."

"But this is different. Daydreaming is wishing for things and knowing they're not true, but playing make-believe is living another life and believing in it and making it *be* true against its will."

"That sounds like Don Quixote."

"No it doesn't. He was just a character in a book."

"Yes, but that's the beauty of it. He was a fictional character who made himself real to a lot of readers. And not only that, there were even some characters in the book itself who thought he was real, too. So when they saw him step out of the pages, he made *them* real as well. He sort of took them along with him, and he breathed life into them and made them happy. He invited them to come along with him on his quest. He gave them an impossible dream to believe in. He gave them something to live for, in other words."

"That was nice. I'd like to know a man like that."

"You could make him up."

"Yes. I suppose I could."

"Tell me something, Sheila. What's the street number of Grosvenor House?"

"It's number 86 Park Lane."

"How do you know that?"

"Mummy told me, when she could still remember it."

"Good grief. How many people in the world know that Grosvenor House is number 86 Park Lane?"

"Is it a secret?"

"No, but most people don't remember the street number of a major hotel. They just remember the name of the hotel itself. They don't really *need* to know the number, so they simply forget it. It's easier that way."

"Why is it easier for people when they forget something they already know?"

I had to smile at the irony of the situation. My mother couldn't remember, and Sheila couldn't forget. Between the two of them they'd lick the platter clean.

I used to worry about how we would take care of Sheila when my mother died, but now I saw that Sheila would be able to take care of herself, for she had slowly learned to deal with the necessities of everyday life as my mother's ability to cope with them had gradually faded away. When I said goodbye to Sheila, I felt a lot better about Mom. She was in good hands, and it went both ways.

CHAPTER TWO

My mother's funeral was a modest one, attended only by family members and a handful of friends. She had lived to be ninety years old, then she had died quietly in her sleep—a babe in the arms of her father, Percy Pond.

I glanced around at the people dotted here and there in the pews, hoping that some latecomers might still turn up.

"Do you think anyone else will be coming?" I asked my husband, knowing he couldn't possibly answer my question.

Gordon shrugged and squeezed my arm, indicating with his chin the sallow, balding minister who had just mounted the raised platform at the front of the chapel. He turned to face his flock, peering at us myopically through his rimless glasses and smiling benevolently at nobody in particular. Then he sat down next to the pulpit and gazed solemnly at his neatly folded hands.

"It's already ten past two," I said anxiously. "I don't think anyone else will be coming. Maybe it's just that Mom has outlived her peers. Not many people make it into their nineties, you know."

Gordon nodded and patted my knee. He wanted to give me reassurance, but at the same time his silence suggested that I ought to stop talking and perhaps join him in a moment of quiet reflection.

After waiting as long as he dared for potential stragglers to fill the pews, the minister finally stood up and approached the pulpit. He greeted us in pleasant, practiced, professional tones, made a few introductory remarks, then continued with some general statements about God's mercy on sinners and our hope for eternal life beyond this vale of tears. His voice had a hollow, portentous quality which echoed through the nearly empty chapel. I settled back in my pew, knowing he'd continue this way for another ten minutes or so. I didn't blame him. My mom hadn't attended many church services, so the minister wasn't acquainted with her and therefore had no choice but to stick to generalities.

I was sorry I hadn't found the time to sit down with him before the funeral and tell him about Mom so he could say something personal about her. But she had died suddenly (if not unexpectedly), and we "children" had all converged on the State of Connecticut from our far-flung homes, feeling stunned, disoriented, and totally unprepared.

As the minister continued commenting on the Bible's message, I thought about what a kind, patient, loving person my mother had been. She had married a passionate, willful, difficult, ambitious, hard-driving, risk-taking, restless man, and had raised six children who were, in many ways, created in their father's image. Nobody but the wisest and most easy-going woman could possibly have put up with six spirited, high-strung children who must have given her many reasons to wring her hands in despair. Yet she had endured us with remarkable equanimity and a splendid sense of humor.

"And now I would like to invite family members to arise and approach the pulpit," the minister said in mellifluous tones, "that you might address your friends and loved ones with recollections about your mother and memories of her life and your lives together as a family."

There was silence in the chapel as we thought about his invitation and attempted to figure out what we might say on the spur of the moment. I looked around, but all heads were bowed. There was no indication that anybody wanted to be the first to answer the minister's call. But somebody had to respond, so I finally got up and made my way to the pulpit, hoping I'd be able to do my mom justice.

When I turned and faced the gathering I was surprised to see that all the heads were now raised, bearing expressions of comfortable anticipation. I began to speak, feeling at home with people I had known all my life.

"What I remember most about Mom was that she was a gentle soul—meek and mild and forgiving. Jesus would have been proud of her. But he had other sides to him, of course, that she never could have lived up to. I mean, I can't even begin to imagine her attacking money changers, for example. She had plenty to say about certain bankers at various points in her life, but I can't see her assaulting them physically.

"I'm not quite sure where I'm going with this, but what I'm trying to say is that what I remember most about Mom was how sweet and kind she was. She was much too good-natured to ever get angry with us, for example. As a matter of fact, she never punished us at all, as far as I can recall. The strongest thing she ever said was... well, I should tell you the whole story first.

"I'll never forget that day, because it was so unlike her to express any sort of disapproval, even the mildest kind. So I was really taken aback when she... Okay, so this is what happened. We were living in Mexico back then. Well, that doesn't have anything to do with the story, but we were in Mexico anyway, and Mom was making dinner for some guests. She was creating this delicious sauce for a poached turbot when she suddenly realized she didn't have enough heavy cream. So she asked Wilda and me to walk down the street to the store and get her some more.

"Well, we went and bought the cream, but as we were going home we began arguing about who should carry it. You know how sisters are. We were stubborn. I figured she was younger than I was, so *she* should carry it. She tossed it to me to get rid of it, and I chucked it back. So we kept flinging it back and forth till the inevitable happened — the bottle finally crashed on the sidewalk. They used glass bottles for milk and cream in those days.

"So we looked at the cream and we looked at each other, then we ran back to the store to get another bottle, but when we got there the place was closed. The windows were barred and nobody was there. They'd all gone home and we were... well, we were dead ducks. There was nothing we could do but go home and tell Mom the truth. Well, not the whole truth. We left out the part about how we were tossing the bottle back and forth. We just told her we'd dropped it by mistake, and now the store was closed and there was nothing we could do. We said we were terribly sorry. We had done our best, but accidents will happen.

"So Mom looked up from the stove, her hair all straggly from sweat and effort, and she said—and this is the strongest thing she's ever said to us in her life—she frowned and she said, 'Oh, children can be so *unsatisfactory* sometimes...'"

That little yarn broke the ice and set the tenor for the rest of the presentations—stories about what a great lady she had been, with such a gentle manner and such a wonderful sense of humor. My brother Nigel (number five in the line-up of six) reminded us that she could imitate any animal you could ever think of, and reproduce a cat fight like nobody else in the world. She'd hide behind the kitchen table when she did that, just to make it even more realistic. She didn't want her audience, after all, to be distracted by her clearly unfeline physical appearance. So Nigel, never one to worry about protocol, promptly crouched behind the pulpit and treated us all to an imitation of Mom's cat fights that was so perfect it brought tears to our eyes.

Then my youngest sister Heather got up (the sixth child) and told us about how she had once put a spider in Mom's powder box. She thought this would be hilariously funny, in view of my mother's incurable arachnophobia. So when my mother opened her powder box that morning, out crawled a spider totally covered in pink powder, right to the tips of its eight hairy little legs. My mother screamed and dropped the powder box. The poor spider ran around frantically trying to find a place to hide, leaving a thin trail of pink powder in its wake. I'm sure Mom thought Heather was more than a little "unsatisfactory" that day, but she didn't get mad at her. All she did was suggest to Heather in the strongest possible way (which wasn't strong at all) that she find a different home for any future spiders she might decide to befriend.

The minister asked my older brother, Craig, if he would like to add anything to the stories, but he declined. We knew he wouldn't want to get up and talk about family anecdotes. He was too intellectual for such things. If you had asked him to explain to you why $E=MC^2$ or how a laser works, he'd have been in his element. He wrote his dissertation on the intricacies of time, space, and relativity. But geniuses don't notice everyday things the way average people do. He had a post graduate degree in nuclear physics from MIT and a PhD from Stanford in mathematics and philosophy, so he was excused from having to notice anything about normal life. As a philosopher he wasn't even sure that things like chairs and tables actually existed anyway, so what can you expect?

As for my older sister Sheila, the firstborn, she was very possibly the smartest one of all the children. But her autism presented certain drawbacks in her perception of reality. She had no doubt that chairs and tables existed, but she hated it when they got moved around or when they weren't perfectly lined up with one another. She was easily upset about their relative place in time, too. If they were not where they were meant to be when she expected them to be there, she would throw herself against the wall in a fit of rage and frustration. Craig was the only one who could soothe her at times like those. He would talk to her about the philosophical and mathematical implications of time, space, and relativity, and this would usually help to take her mind off the unbearably random quality of life as it really was.

As far as I was concerned, my mother's chairs and tables would forever remind me of where she used to sit and what she used to say when we were together. Her chair would be empty now, a poignant reminder of days gone by. But her presence would remain—silent and powerful and mixed with the echoes of eternity. I could almost hear the lyrical tenor voice of young Marius as he sang his heartrending aria about empty chairs at empty tables in *Les Misérables:*

> *There's a grief that can't be spoken.*
> *There's a pain goes on and on.*
> *Empty chairs at empty tables*
> *Now my friends are dead and gone.*

When we had finished our reminiscences about life with Mom, the minister got up and asked if there was anyone else who wished to add to the *encomia* that had been offered to her that day. We all knew that Sheila had been excused. It never would have occurred to her to address the audience anyway.

"*I* have something to say," said a trembling voice from the back of the room.

We all turned around and stared, but we weren't sure who had spoken.

"Yes?" said the minister. "Please come forward."

An elderly gentleman began struggling to his feet. He was tall, slender, and well coifed, with rugged, handsome features, but he looked as though he had known better days. His rumpled suit was a size too large, and had clearly started out with a different owner. Either that, or the present owner had lost a fair bit of weight. The woman next to him handed him his cane and helped him come to the front of the chapel. The minister took over from there, and assisted him up the stairs and around to the pulpit. The old gentleman cleared his throat and gave the mike a couple of taps, then he blinked timidly at the audience.

"I'm an old friend of your mother's," he began, without introducing himself. "I go all the way back to the days when her name was Marion Belle Pond. I know she doesn't like to be called Marion Belle anymore, so I've learned to call her Heather. This is the name she has chosen for herself, but I'm afraid that name doesn't make any sense. She'll always be Marion Belle to me. That's what she was called when she was at 16 Divisadero Street in San Francisco. She lived there with her mother, Harriet Hall Pond, and her brother, Edwin Percy Pond, Jr."

As I listened to his faltering words, I tried to remember what my mother had told me about her life in San Francisco. I knew that Edwin was an invalid with a "weak heart" who worked at home under his mother's watchful eye. He wasn't allowed to leave the house or exert himself in any way in case he should suffer a fatal heart attack. My grandmother hovered over him incessantly, doing everything she could to keep him safe and lengthen his life as much as possible. Various friends would come over to the house to keep Edwin company and to help my grandmother take care of him, but I couldn't remember any of their names.

"I fell in love with Marion Belle after the First World War," he continued, looking at us apologetically. "That's why I can't call her Heather. Heather isn't her real name. I can't understand why she changed her name to Heather. It would be just as strange if Annabelle Lee had changed her name to something like Holly or Clover in mid poem."

I glanced surreptitiously at baby Heather, as we used to call my youngest sister in the days when I was teaching her to walk. She was sitting there looking noncommittal and slightly uneasy, hoping people wouldn't crane their necks and stare at her, just as I was doing. I turned around again and focused my attention on the mysterious old gentleman.

"Marion Belle was the love of my life," he was saying, "and she sustained me in my walk through the valley of the shadow of death. Marion Belle was an angel. There's no other word for her. She was an angel."

He paused for a moment, then gave a heavy sigh.

It was many and many a year ago,
In a kingdom in the dell,

That a maiden there lived whom you may know
By the name of Marion Belle;
And this maiden she lived with no other thought
Than to love and be loved as well.

At this point in his story we were all sitting there frozen in place, wondering what he was going to say next, mortified by the embarrassing confessions we might have to listen to that afternoon. There was a pause, and I looked up just in time to see him wiping away a tear with the back of his hand. He was unhurried about it, and not in the least bit ashamed.

"They call it *shell shock* nowadays," he continued. "But back then they just called it *grief.* All I know is that after I saw my buddies blown to pieces I had no more desire to live. It was all too horrible to even describe. I can barely bring myself to think about the war, even today. I tried to join my buddies in the great hereafter by doing some heroics that would get me killed. But God had other ideas. He wouldn't let me die, no matter what I did. All I saw was more death and carnage, more boys dying, until I couldn't take it anymore, and… and then I began to think about Marion Belle. She was my angel of mercy."

The minister had approached the pulpit and was gently trying to guide him down the stairs.

"Wait, I haven't finished yet," the old gentleman said.

"It's time to go," the minister remarked, in a kind, firm voice. "The funeral service is over now."

"It is? I'm sorry. I didn't know." His trembling fingers grasped his cane. "I guess I talk too much sometimes. I've never been able to tell a story in a concise manner. They're always too long. Either I say too much or I say nothing at all. I can't seem to find the right words to express what I really feel. It's too complicated. It's just… too difficult."

Shell shock, I was thinking. *Shell shock.* My mother had told me about an old friend from Juneau who had gotten shell shock in the First World War. What was his name?

As the minister was leading him away, my mother's old friend suddenly stopped short and looked up at the ceiling. "Marion Belle!" he cried out. "You don't need me to put it all into words. You understand. I know you do. You've always understood. Please say a prayer for me. Pray for me, Marion Belle. God listens to his angels!"

By this time the minister had escorted him to the back of the chapel. They seemed to be talking with each other, but nobody could hear what they were saying. Then another old man in the last pew got up and joined the conversation, but he was too far away for me to see him clearly. The three of them talked for a little while, then the minister opened the door, letting in a narrow shaft of light, and the two elderly gentlemen walked out into the sunlight.

Something strange happened at that point. I suddenly felt my mother's presence in the chapel, and I had the strong impression that she had heard and savored every word we had said about her in our anecdotes and reminiscences. Her old friend must have felt her, too. He surely knew that she had looked on him with an understanding built of love and deep respect. I knew she was seeing all of us that way. It wasn't an eerie or ghostly sensation, of course, but a tender, reassuring feeling that she was still lingering there with us, smiling fondly and shaking her head at all the mischief we had hidden from her over the years.

I wish I could have left it at that. But when the moment came for us to bow our heads and meditate silently about Mom, I felt a rush of sorrow for the time I could have shared with her but chose, instead, to spend on my own pursuits or on my immediate family. I knew I could have been a better daughter. I could have given her more joy, and shared more moments with her. But when I was young I was too callow, and when I grew older I was too busy.

I felt her presence clearly as I sat there in the pew. I missed her terribly, but most of all I needed her forgiveness. There was one episode in particular that gave me a feeling of deep shame and regret when I looked back on it. But I didn't have to ask her to forgive me, for she was close by, already offering her pardon in the same way she gave me everything else I had ever needed—with wholehearted generosity and unconditional love.

As we all filed silently out the front door of the chapel, I looked about to see if I could spot the old gentleman lurking somewhere. Would he be waiting in the parking lot for us? I wanted to meet him, this man who had loved my mother all his life. I was curious to know what he could tell me about my Uncle Edwin, the talented graphic artist who had to work at home so as not to strain his heart. But is it really possible to protect a heart just by keeping it at home? Does it never quicken at the thought of love, or leap with excitement when gaining new insights, or making new discoveries, or learning to connect the dots in the world beyond?

Maybe my mother's old admirer would know, I thought. He had been my uncle's close friend, right up to the moment he had died. Maybe there were things he could tell me about both my uncle and my mother. I found myself yearning to see her through the eyes of the man who had loved her so deeply and so faithfully for so long.

I looked around the parking lot, but there was no sign of him or the other elderly gentleman who had left the chapel with him. I was worried that he might be feeling desolate and lonely, having lost, through my mom's death, his fragile lifeline to hope. Then again, maybe I was projecting my own feelings onto him. It was unfair of me to do that, of course, since my experience of life didn't come close to matching his. I had never suffered from shell shock. My close friends had never been blown to pieces in front of my eyes. I had never been perceived as someone who needed to be gently escorted out of a chapel.

CHAPTER THREE

After the funeral service in the chapel in Greenwich, Connecticut, the town where we children had spent most of our teenage and pre-teenage years after World War II, I found myself thinking about my mother almost every day. I missed her, and it hurt. My greatest comfort at that time was the thick pile of letters that she had sent me in my student years. They had all been written with a fountain pen on onion skin paper, representing infinite hours of hard work and faithful love. She had written most of them between 1955 and 1966, a period that had started shortly before I graduated from the Greenwich Academy and ended while I was studying for my PhD at Harvard, but they had trailed off as Alzheimer's slowly began to take hold. She would begin one thing and then get side-tracked and plunge into something else, so she was never able to finish anything she started. She did write me letters, though, and I answered all of them.

I was particularly struck by one of the letters she wrote me in the summer of 1966. It seems to summarize perfectly my sudden desire to visit all her old haunts and to meet the people she loved and who meant so much to her at various points in her life.

My daughter is in Madrid somewhere, swinging around on a motor scooter. Does it make you feel nostalgic? A revisit to a place always does that to me, and there's hurt that goes with it that's hard to describe—a consortium with old ghosts, a longing, sometimes illogically, to get them all back, just as they were, and there to remain until the end of time! With that wish comes dire frustration. There's no way we can be at all the old places again, living with every ghost we ever knew—those of childhood, early youth, and for me the joyful ghosts of the child-bearing and child-rearing age, all the folks who were interested and who meant so much to me at the time, as though this phase could remain forever and we'd always find life an intensely exciting adventure.

Yet where are they now? I make an effort, sometimes, to keep in touch with my old friends, but I confess it's half-hearted most of the time, which must be a reflection on myself —my own remissness and procrastination.

I think you've sensed this sadness somehow, which may become more poignant as the years march on. You'll have it if you pass your old apartment in Madrid and feel like going in, probably thinking, "It's Gill's night to cook. I wonder what she'll make, and will Carlos be pleased?" But now the play is over, and all the characters are gone. Gill is back in England, and Carlos has taken his final curtain. As the French say, "tout passe," and oh, how quickly! I guess that's why we feel we must hang on as tightly as possible. It's funny, when we look back on our lives we tend to remember people more than anything else, and to a lesser extent what we learned, what we saw, and what we did.

I can understand the yearning we all have to go back to our roots, hoping to meet the people who shared our lives in those old times and places. My mother was right when she said that it's a poignant, delightful feeling to be close to them in that way. There are those who maintain, however, that we idealize people and exaggerate their virtues when we conjure them up in our memories. We see them through rose-colored glasses, and remember them as better than they really were.

But I think it's entirely possible that the opposite is true. We tend to undervalue the people who live with us and share our lives on an everyday basis. We take them for granted and even neglect them sometimes as we keep our eyes fixed on the intriguing opportunities that await us at the end of the next rainbow. Before we know it all those people are gone, and suddenly we remember them as indeed they really were, with all the virtues that we had no time to appreciate, or that we were too selfish to notice.

We don't really look back on them through rose-colored glasses—the truth is that we saw them through dim, smoke-colored glasses while they were alive. But when the scales fall off our eyes we often make the mistake of refusing to wear our rose-colored glasses lest we be perceived as overly sentimental or misguided by wishful thinking. So we let our golden chances pass us by, to quote one of my favorite songs from *Carousel.*

The terrible thing is that the people we care about the most will indeed go off in the mist of day, never to know how we loved them. So if the nostalgia of looking back over time is painful, the regret of having neglected to show and express our love is even worse. I don't think my mother ever knew how much I loved her, and this feeling makes me want to visit *her* old haunts, to find her house in San Francisco, and visit her birthplace in Juneau, and return to 49 Charles Street where we all lived together in London.

What was it like growing up in Juneau? Who did Mom know there? I knew my grandmother quite well, but what was my grandfather like? Who was Percy Pond? My mother often spoke to me about him, describing him as a dreamy, impractical, artistically talented man who made a rather meager living as a photographer. He was a poetic soul, according to her, and a consummate outdoorsman. He and his partner, Lloyd Winter, were always tramping around in the frozen hinterland carrying tripods and heavy cameras and massive glass plates. But she never heard her dad complain about the cold or the discomfort of living with frostbite and having only biscuits and beef jerky and snow to eat while he was out trekking, forever looking for new ways to capture the spirit of Alaska through the lens of his camera.

Percy Pond had been lured up to Alaska from his home in San Francisco back in 1893, when he was only twenty-one years old. His best friend, a first-class swimmer and portrait painter by the name of Lloyd Winter, had convinced him that Seward's Folly was not so foolish after all, and was in dire need of being photographed for posterity. And so it was that the two young men decided to travel north to explore this frosty new piece of American real estate.

Five years later Percy went back down to San Francisco and married his sweetheart, Harriet Hall, a young San Francisco socialite whom he had met at the Winter Cotillion, and where they had danced the night away in each other's arms. Miss Hall, petite and raven-haired with flashing black eyes, had been described as "the belle of the ball," while Mr. Pond—tall, blond, and athletic—was known for his prowess as a swimmer and California State diving champion.

But it is a rare belle who can brave a hell like the frozen north, so when Percy told his bride about his glorious dreams of life in the American frontier, my grandmother greeted his stories with downright skepticism. She was not at all certain that Alaska was the place for her. Opposites attract, however, and love eventually prevailed, so Percy Pond returned to his budding photography business in Juneau, Alaska with his grumbling young bride in tow.

He and Lloyd Winter had set up shop in a clapboard house on Front Street, which at that time was no more than a muddy road lined with wooden planks. Percy Pond was undaunted, however, and painted a large sign informing the residents of Juneau that *Winter and Pond, Photographers* was open for business.

The two hopeful young partners waited and waited, but sales didn't come rolling in quite the way they had expected. They added some Indian curiosities, carvings, totems, silver, baskets, and other items to their inventory, hoping the more varied product line-up would increase sales, but their total income failed to satisfy the redoubtable Harriet Hall, who was now pregnant with baby Edwin. Her habitual grumbling increased as she began to realize, to her great dismay, that her options in life were diminishing along with her prospects of ever returning to the lower forty-eight.

Percy and Lloyd, meanwhile, had befriended the Tlingit and Haida Indians, whose art and culture fascinated them. Lloyd, a linguistically gifted man, even learned to speak the language of the Chilkat tribe. They took many photos of their leaders, their families, their artwork, their ceremonial dress, their villages and totem poles—becoming veritable anthropologists in their own right.

Hattie Hall observed these developments with unveiled indignation.

"Why do you spend so much time taking photographs of those people?" she would ask her husband, her arms folded over her chest and standing as tall as her 5'1" frame would permit. "They're not going to put bread on the table! How do you expect me to feed little Edwin? What am I supposed to give him? Whale blubber?"

There was no question about it—poor Lloyd Winter and Percy Pond were living a hand-to-mouth existence in a cold, harsh, inhospitable climate, and Harriet Hall was not to that manner born. Her spirits dropped even more when, five years after Edwin was born, she found herself pregnant once again. On November 7th, 1904, she gritted her teeth and gave birth to baby Marion Belle.

"I was freezing cold from the very moment I was born," my mother would complain to me later. "I never thawed out until we left Alaska, when I was ten years old."

I have to applaud my grandmother for sticking it out in Alaska for more than two decades. She had her faults like all the rest of us, but she was a woman of character, and she had made a commitment to her husband that she fully intended to honor. But there is one thing that can make even the most principled woman disregard her solemn promise to stay by her husband's side, and that is her concern for the welfare of her child. Maternal love is a visceral, desperate, feral sort of instinct that pushes aside every other kind of love, especially when a child is in crisis.

And so it was that when Edwin woke up with an earache one cold winter morning, my grandmother ministered to him with more anxiety than she normally would have felt if she had been living in more favorable circumstances. Her 21 years in Alaska had taught her that a sick child is always in serious danger, so she had sent for the doctor immediately. After due consideration, he counseled my grandmother to pour warm oil in the young man's ear and to call him back in a day or so if the trouble persisted.

Who could have imagined that the best thing would have been to take a sharp instrument and pierce Edwin's eardrum to let all the pus drain out? Such drastic measures are never considered until after the fact, when it's too late to go back and retrace one's steps. Nobody realized that the pus would be forced to empty inward into his bloodstream. He was fortunate to have survived this terrible bout of mastoiditis, but the poison corroded his heart valves so badly that the doctor gave him no more than a year to live.

"When Granny heard the news," my mother told me many years later, "she ran to her room and slammed the door. Then she gave a howl that was as long and drawn out as the wolf cries we used to hear in the night, coming from the woods around Juneau. It was terrible. I felt chills all up and down my spine. I had never known her to lose control before. She was the strongest woman in the world, believe me, but even the toughest women have their limits. When you love with all your heart, you're capable of feeling pain right to the core or your being. So when you have a child, you're vulnerable to the possibility of unthinkable pain for the rest of your life. Fortunately most of us don't dwell on this. In fact, we don't even know what a precarious position we're in. So when an accident or an illness takes you to the very brink, then the doors are opened and you *know*, and this is a terrible thing. A curse. You live with the knowing and you worry constantly about your children. But *they* don't know. They just prance around taking chances and merrily risking their lives or their basic welfare, while you wait for your turn to join the wolves in the night."

We both fell silent for a while, thinking about the vale of tears from our different perspectives.

"So then what happened, Mom?" I asked.

I'd heard the story before, but she always told me some little detail that she had overlooked on previous occasions.

"Well, my mother was determined to get Edwin some proper medical care, so in 1914 she packed us up and moved us down to San Francisco, where she had the right contacts to see to it that Edwin was well taken care of."

"How old were you both at that time?"

"Edwin was fifteen, and I was ten."

"So what did you do for money? How did you support yourselves in San Francisco?"

"My mother became a school teacher, and she found a tutor for Edwin so he could stay home. He was the son of a mining engineer in Juneau, so they already knew each other. They used to play together as boys."

"What was he like, this tutor?"

"He was tall, with a sensitive face—a handsome face. He looked sort of like Lord Byron. He had dark, thoughtful, understanding eyes."

"Did you love him?"

My mother gave a quick laugh.

"Teenagers love anyone who looks like Byron."

"How did your father feel, being left behind? I know he couldn't have felt very happy about it, but was he absolutely devastated, do you think? Was he all torn apart?"

My mother sat there and thought for a while before she answered me.

"It must have been the hardest decision of his life," she said finally. "On the one hand, he wanted what was best for his son. Paternal love is powerfully strong, too, but men show it in a different way. They don't seem to feel that their *presence* in a person's life is as important as their ability to provide sustenance and opportunities and security to their families. And there lies the rub. My dad, I think, felt that he had failed us miserably. He was never very good at bringing home the bacon. It wasn't as though he didn't care, but life was difficult in a frontier town, and the climate didn't help much, either. You have to remember that he had a business that wasn't exactly tailor-made for raking in the dough.

"The business had its ups and downs, of course. There was a time when things went a little better for us, when Bart Thane built the dam up at Salmon Creek and constructed a hydroelectric plant that supplied Juneau with electricity year round. He also started up some gold mines in the area, and he asked my father to take photos of them. This all happened during the Klondike Gold Rush, so there were a lot of miners passing through Juneau. Anyway, Uncle Bart paid my father well for his work, and they became close friends. His wife was also a great friend of my mother's, and their daughter always played with me. Big Fay and Little Fay, we called them. Those were happy times for us, but it didn't last long. Edwin developed his heart trouble and my mother decided to move down to San Francisco.

"I have to admit that my mother couldn't forgive my father for being such an unsatisfactory provider, and he couldn't forgive himself, either. Sometimes the trouble in a family comes from the one who feels like the greatest failure. My mother never gave up on him for twenty-one years, but he was always finding reasons to go somewhere far away to take his pictures so he wouldn't have to face her reproachful brown eyes.

"He always believed he'd eventually get paid for all his labor. It never occurred to him that most people think that photographers and writers and creative people in general are just working to please themselves, and they shouldn't really have to be paid for their work, since in their opinion it's not really work at all. To them it's just a form of egotistical self-indulgence on the part of someone who never grew up, who could never land a *real* job—one that brings in a regular paycheck. On top of that, people feel that if they know the artist, they should be given his work for nothing. So I guess we'll always have garrets."

"Do you think everyone would have been better off if your dad had gone with you to San Francisco?" I asked her, hoping to stay away from the subject of poverty and garrets and the miserable sense of failure that accompanies them.

"Well, my dad always said he couldn't let Lloyd down. They'd put twenty years into their business, and it was bound to succeed very soon. He couldn't justify starting again from scratch, but my mother always said it wouldn't have made any difference, since ten times nothing is still nothing."

"She wasn't very encouraging, was she?"

"She had her edgy side, I know. But who can blame her? Twenty years is a long time to keep nurturing a business that is forever teetering on the brink. She was pretty brave to put up with it as long as she did. But in those days women stood by their men, even if they did nag them a lot. My mother never would have dreamed of packing up and going back to San Francisco if it hadn't been for Edwin."

"I can understand that."

"There was another reason too," my mother added. "I always thought it had something to do with Uncle Bart. He was a true and loyal friend. One of the few you can count on the fingers of one hand, as Granny used to say. If it hadn't been for him, I don't know what we would have done."

"What was he like?"

"He had the Midas touch, that man. He had that rare combination of energy, common sense, good planning, and intelligence. Wisdom, too. And all those good qualities were combined with compassion and generosity and a concern for public welfare. Granny always said that he brought Juneau

into the twentieth century. He was an extremely successful
financier and a great entrepreneur, and all at such a young
age, too. He wasn't much older than my father."

"You said a minute ago that if it hadn't been for Bart
Thane, you don't know what you would have done. What did
you mean by that?"

"Well, my dad didn't like to talk about this, but Uncle
Bart saw how hard he and Lloyd Winter were struggling, so
he made the photography business into a corporation and
bought into it himself. He contributed a lot of money to it,
which kept us all going."

"It doesn't sound like a very good deal for Bart Thane."

"It wasn't, of course. He did it out of the goodness of his
heart, knowing full well he'd never get anything back on his
investment. That's why we were all so grateful to him. He
went on funding us, even when the money kept pouring
down the drain."

"Maybe he got a tax write-off," I ventured.

"I don't know about that," Mom said. "I don't really
know how a thing like that would work. But what I do know
is that when Granny took Edwin and me with her to San
Francisco, your grandfather felt he had to stay behind and try
to make the business work so he could help to repay Uncle
Bart. So you see, it was very difficult for him to make up his
mind about what to do. He was torn between staying with his
family on the one hand, and paying back Uncle Bart and
being fair to Lloyd on the other. But I was much too young
to understand the kind of dilemma he was facing. I was only
ten years old. All I knew was that we were going to San
Francisco and he was staying in Juneau, and I didn't understand why he couldn't come with us..."

Her voice trailed off as she thought about that painful
separation from her father.

"It's ironic, isn't it?" she continued. "Uncle Bart wanted
to help, but what happened was that the family got separated
because of his generosity. Well, partly because of it."

"So how long did he keep on financing the company?"

"It's such a heart-rending story. He made a business trip to New York and caught influenza and died suddenly, in just a day or two. He died all alone in his hotel room, with nobody there to attend him. Auntie Fay and Aunt Laura were heartbroken. And Little Fay too, of course. He was such a young man—only in his thirties. It was just tragic."

"That's so sad, Mom."

"It was. After that my father and Lloyd Winter had an even harder time financially, if such a thing is possible. They had to borrow on their life insurance just to survive. My dad went panning for gold every chance he had, but he never got anywhere with that, either."

"You must have missed Primrose very much."

"Primrose…" she smiled. "You remember our pet name for him! I've always thought of him as *Primrose*."

"Whose idea was it to call him that?"

"It was Edwin's idea. We had a language all of our own when we were children."

"That's true. You've always called dogs *negwooties,* and cats *geetzes,* and horses *anyahs,* and ducks *nuckety anns...*"

"Yes. We thought the names we chose captured the very essence of those annies."

"You've always called animals *annies,* too."

"That was also Edwin's idea. He believed that when he named the animals, they belonged to him somehow. They became truly his. He used to love that feeling."

"Maybe that's why God gave Adam that job."

"I expect so. I never thought of it that way."

"So did Primrose ever visit you in San Francisco?"

My mother gave a quick chuckle.

"Good heavens, no. There were no planes in those days, and it took the steamers a very long time to make the trip."

"You must have missed him a lot."

"I did, with all my heart," she said, looking down at her lap. "I can understand why my mother had to leave Alaska, though. Edwin was really very frail, with his heart condition. You could hear the sound of the blood swishing around in his poor, damaged heart. He probably would have died much sooner if he'd stayed on in Juneau. But I missed my father more than anything in the world. I always dreamed of leaving San Francisco and going back to Alaska to live with him for the rest of my life."

"For the rest of *his* life, you mean."

"You're right, but I never really thought he'd die. Well, I knew he would, of course, but that was never on my mind. I just wanted to be with him, and have him all to myself, and talk to him about grownup things, and just be happy. But then I met Daddy, *your* daddy I mean, and after that all those dreams went up in smoke."

"Why don't *you* go to Alaska, then? Why don't you go there and visit all your old haunts, as you call them? You've always said you'd like to do that. Why don't you go? It'd give you something to do."

"I'd like to, but I hate the idea of traveling alone. I don't like to travel unless I have someone to talk to. It's sad to see things and go places without having anyone to share it with."

She hesitated a moment. I knew what she was thinking, and I hoped she wouldn't say it.

"Why don't *you* come along, dear? I'd pay for our trip, of course. Seeing Juneau would be so much more fun for me if I could share it with you. We'd have a grand time!"

"Mom, you know I can't go. I'm a teaching assistant at the University of California, your alma mater. I have classes to give and papers to grade. And I have to prepare for my MA finals. I can't just up and leave."

I hated my tense, apologetic tone. It sounded whiny.

"It's all right, darling. I know how busy you are. Don't worry. We'll go to Alaska together some day, you'll see. We just don't know yet when that will be."

CHAPTER FOUR

Gordon and I were sitting at the breakfast table in Lunenburg, Nova Scotia. It was a Saturday morning, and all was well with the world. The year was anno domini 1998. Our daughter Valerie was 27, and in her second year as a medical student at Columbia University's College of Physicians and Surgeons. Vicki was 24, married, with an art degree from Calvin College, and running her own business—a print shop in Grand Rapids called *The Printer's Inc.* Our company, *Peninsula Farm*, was selling a good share of the yogurt consumed in Nova Scotia, and Blair Landry was doing an excellent job as the general manager. I had retired as Chairperson of the Department of Spanish at Dalhousie University. We were free.

I could see the top of Gordon's head peeking up over his newspaper.

"Gordon, I've been thinking…"

He put the newspaper down and peered at me with his *"Uh oh, what now?"* expression.

"It's been three years since my mom died," I continued. "She never did have the opportunity to go back to Alaska."

"That's probably a good thing. Didn't you tell me one time that she hated the cold?"

"Yes, but that wouldn't have been a problem. She could have gone in the summer time."

"Well, why didn't she?"

"She wanted to go with someone. She didn't want to go alone. She wanted to share all the excitement with someone she cared about. Someone who could be excited, too."

"You're good at being excited. Why didn't *you* go?"

"She wanted me to. She asked me to go with her once. She even offered to pay for my trip, too."

"That sounds good. Why didn't you take her up on it?"

"Three guesses. I've been just a wee bit busy for most of my life. I didn't have time to go with her then. But I regret it now. She could have told me so many interesting details about her life in Alaska, and now I suppose I'll never know the whole story."

"That's too bad, Hon. Really it is." He picked up the paper and began to read again.

"You and I could go this summer."

The newspaper landed on the table with a loud rustle. Gordon's expression was one of unequivocal alarm.

"What are you cooking up *now?*"

"There's no reason we can't go. I've been giving it a lot of thought. Everything's under control. We should just go while the going's good. Why wait till things get even more complicated and more inconvenient?"

"We can't just drop everything here and go waltzing off to Juneau, Alaska, of all places."

"Give me one good reason why we can't."

He lined up all his objections in a neat little row, and I shot them down, one by one. I felt like Ethel Merman in *Annie, Get Your Gun.*

It took me a couple of weeks to figure out the details and make the arrangements, but on a bright August morning in 1998, we set out at last to visit the land of my mother's birth. We took an Air Canada flight to Vancouver, and from there we boarded a Princess cruise ship to Alaska.

It turned out to be one of the most glorious, informative, touching, picturesque cruises of our lives. We did "the tourist thing," of course, but what a treat it was just to lie back and be taken by ship, bus and train to all the most interesting locations, accompanied by a lively, attractive, athletic, well-informed young woman whose job it was to make sure we were happy and comfortable every inch of the way! We've been on many fine cruises in the past, but I have to say that the Australians and the Alaskans treat tourists to the best times of their lives. I wouldn't have hesitated for a moment to hire any one of those enthusiastic young guides to work for me at Peninsula Farm, our dairy product manufacturing company in Nova Scotia. They had all the qualities that a business owner looks for: intelligence, high spirits, and an innate ability to handle general confusion with patience, confidence, and a sensitive understanding of human nature.

Even though the Australians and the Alaskans are on opposite ends of the globe, I had the feeling that they had a lot in common. They are a pioneer people, and they've had to deal with extreme weather and harsh conditions in order to scratch out a living in their respective lands. They've fought hard-won battles in the past, and the descendants of the survivors have a certain *can-do* attitude that I find appealing. They're down-to-earth, optimistic, not easily intimidated, and quick to take up a challenge. They work hard, laugh a lot, and judging from the significant number of cute little taverns we visited, they do their fair share of drinking, too. But that, as they say, goes with the territory. Like many other people whose natural habitats are severe and unforgiving, Aussies and Alaskans are quick to help their neighbors, and they know how to share whatever blessings they manage to tease out of the reticent earth.

It would be disingenuous of me not to mention the fact, at this particular point in the story, that my father was born in Melbourne, Australia, and brought up in Perth, a beautiful port city on the other side of the continent. My impressions of our new friends in Alaska made me wonder if my father, somewhere deep in his heart, felt some kind of kinship with my mother that he didn't exactly know how to explain.

On further reflection, however, I had to admit that if this was the case it probably had very little to do with the pioneer spirit I've just described. When I think back on their stories, it occurs to me that neither my mother nor my father felt at home in their native lands. Granted, my mother missed her dad and wanted to go back to Juneau to be with him, but she didn't miss Alaska *per se*. As for my father, he had no great sympathy for his native land, which struck him as rather primitive and behind the times when he was growing up in Perth. There were, no doubt, certain small pockets of culture dotted here and there on the landscape like the rare and beautiful wild flowers that grow in spite of everything in the dry, red Australian earth. But this would not have been enough to satisfy my father, who had very little patience for what he used to describe as the rampant mediocrity that flourished unchecked in Australia back in those days. So when, as a boy of fifteen, he was offered a job as a sort of stand-up comedian on a ship bound for Europe, he jumped at the opportunity. It struck me as rather sad and not a little poignant that neither of my parents ever returned to the lands of their birth.

The Sun Princess docked in Juneau at seven o'clock in the morning on a beautiful day. Gordon and I hung over the railing of the deck and drank in the sight of the place that had been home to my mother and her family for so many years. It lay stretched out at the foot of Mount Juneau, a forbidding precipice that peered down over the city from an altitude of about 4,000 feet, like a hungry giant ready to swallow up the human ants that were busily going about their usual daily business in the downtown area. Planted atop this looming mountain is the massive Mendenhall Glacier, which takes sadistic pleasure in chilling the winds that slide over its surface as they swoop down on the shivering, blue-nosed population of Juneau in winter time.

The average daily temperature is actually not really that cold in Juneau as compared to what it's like in the rest of the state, but my mother always spoke in such convincing terms about how close she came to turning into a veritable ice maiden that it forever colored my perception of the weather there. I have no doubt that the conditions at the time she lived there were fairly primitive, and therefore she probably underwent real suffering because of the lack of creature comforts in her house. But she also was known to suffer from low blood pressure all her life, so her extremities were always tinged a light blue in spite of her propensity in later life to turn up the thermostat at the slightest provocation.

Our guide told us over breakfast that Juneau had been built on a slag heap consisting of the tailings of the many gold mines that had been dug out from the foot of the cliff.

"Do you know," she said, buttering another piece of toast, "that Juneau is the only capital city in the world that's not accessible by land? Yes, it's true. Nobody can leave or enter Juneau except by sea or air. The cars and trucks you see in the streets have been brought in by ferry. So the city has been both protected and isolated ever since old Joe Juneau founded the place when the miners first came here. He was the co-founder, actually, with another man called Richard Harris."

"Tell us about this Joe Juneau," somebody piped up.

"He was a gold prospector from Quebec. He became friendly with a local Tlingit chieftain called Kowee, who showed him where he could find gold in this area. He did pretty well here, but eventually he pulled up stakes and went to Dawson City, where he later died of pneumonia."

Our guide continued to sketch out a general picture of Juneau for us, including some interesting bits of information such as the fact that the borough of Juneau is the second largest city in the United States as far as area is concerned—it's about the same size as Puerto Rico, or Delaware and Rhode Island combined, but it has only a little over 30,000 inhabitants, mostly clustered in the downtown area.

My father, the self-appointed arbiter of the world's mediocrity factor, would have been very pleased to know that Juneau now boasts two opera houses, with performances in English and Italian; a symphony orchestra; a professional theater (the only one in Alaska); and dozens of art galleries, as well as some excellent museums and libraries. Juneau also hosts the Alaska Folk Festival and the Juneau Jazz and Classics Music Festival, as well as open-air music and dance performances at Marine Park in the summertime. There are also fifteen schools in Juneau, including an alternative high school and a home-schooling program, and the University of Alaska Southeast has its main campus there. By the time our guide had finished her informative introduction, I was ready to move to Juneau and spend the rest of my life on Front St.

"Do you think they might need a Spanish professor at the University of Alaska Southeast?" I asked Gordon.

"You've already done that. You wouldn't want to go all the way back to square one again, would you?"

"I suppose not. But it seems like a place where people would connect with Don Quixote. You'd have to be a crazy romantic to live up here, it seems to me."

"I don't think you'd find it so romantic after a while," Gordon said.

"Perhaps not. But that's in the very nature of what it means to be romantic. It's more suited to the mind than it is to real life. I'm a bookworm, after all. I live in my head."

"Nonsense. I've never heard of a romantic who could run a successful business."

"That's because there are two different characters living inside me. One is like my dad, Kay Harrison, and the other one is like my mom and like Percy Pond."

"Well, let's go and find out something about Percy Pond before you decide to adopt him as one of your alter egos."

We finished our coffee and disembarked. I felt gripped by a sensation of poignancy and indescribable yearning that I found both exciting and mysterious. My feet were now on the hallowed ground my mother had trod, along with Hattie Hall, and Percy Pond, and my uncle Edwin. I could feel the presence of Uncle Bart Thane, and his wife Big Fay, and their daughter, Little Fay. These were the "old haunts" that my mother talked about, and the ghosts were all around.

I was struck by the peculiar notion that the places in this world where I could best indulge my feelings of nostalgia were now starting to multiply by geometric progression. Not only did I have a list of locales that gave me that ineffable feeling of yearning—places where I had lived for a year or more such as London (England), Berkeley (California), Greenwich (Connecticut), Bennington (Vermont), Madrid, Mexico City, Paris, Cambridge (Massachusetts), Halifax, and Lunenburg (Nova Scotia), but I was now adding my mother's special haunts to my list as well. By the time I finished with her and my dad and my grandparents on both sides, I'd be a cauldron of bubbling nostalgia, wanting to be everywhere at once and yearning for it all to last forever.

"Look over there!" Gordon exclaimed, as we stepped off the gangplank. "See that little cabin, or whatever it is?"

"The one that says *Tourist Information* over the door?"

"Yes. Let's go in there and see if they can help us."

I approached the woman at the main desk and asked her if she could tell me anything about the old days in Juneau.

"Is there something in particular you'd like to know?"

"Well, I was wondering if you could tell me about a man who settled here back in 1893. His name was Percy Pond."

"Oh. That's a rather tall order. I don't know too much about the specifics. I could give you a general outline of the history, but I'm not familiar with the individuals who lived here that long ago. Did you say 1893? That's over a hundred years ago. I'm afraid it's a bit before my time."

"Right. Well, do you know where I could find out?"

"How long did he live here? Did he stay here a while?"

"Yes, he lived here until he died, in 1943."

"I tell you what. See that elderly lady sitting over there by the window? She's 97 years old. She might remember the man you're interested in."

"Thanks. I'll go talk to her."

Now that I was doing the math, I was astonished at how young my grandfather had been when he'd packed up all his belongings and set out for parts unknown. Percy Pond was just 21 when he moved to Alaska, and Lloyd Winter was only six years older than he was. Yet they'd had the courage to throw themselves recklessly into an unknown world with nothing to depend on or to fall back on but their own wits, and hard work and determination. To make things even more difficult, Percy was married to a woman who expected to be well cared-for by her husband. It must have been daunting for a twenty-one-year-old who as yet had so little experience or knowledge of the world.

I approached the old lady in question and smiled at her. She looked at me sharply and said nothing. She didn't return my smile, either, so I decided to just plunge right in without any introductions or fanfare.

"I was wondering if you happened to know a man who lived here in Juneau around the turn of the century."

Before I could even mention his name she was already telling me that *lots* of men lived in Juneau around the turn of the century, and if I expected her to remember him it would be extremely helpful if I could supply her with a name.

"He was called Percy Pond," I said, realizing it would be wise to come straight to the point in my conversation with this woman.

"Who? Pond the photographer?"

"Yes!" I said, delighted. "Do you remember him?"

"Of course I remember him. Why wouldn't I?" she said testily.

It began to dawn on me that she was probably used to being treated as though she were slightly deaf or slow-witted because of her age, so she had learned to come out fighting like a cornered timber wolf.

"So, were you a friend of his?" I asked her.

"Now why would I be a friend of a man who was old enough to be my *father*? Of course I wasn't a friend of his. I just knew who he was. Everybody knew who he was."

"This is so exciting!" I said breathlessly.

"What's exciting about it?"

"Well, it's so wonderful to meet someone who knew my grandfather."

"Percy Pond was your grandfather? Well, why didn't you say so? Why didn't you tell me that in the first place?"

"I don't know. I was getting to it, I suppose."

"He had a daughter called Marion Belle."

"Yes! That was my mother's name! Marion Belle!"

"Well I should certainly hope that you'd know your own mother's name. That shouldn't come as any surprise to you. Marion Belle used to come to my father's butcher counter every Saturday to buy meat."

"Were you a friend of my mother's, then?"

"No. She was three years younger than I was. At that age you're not interested in other children who are that much younger than you are."

"I suppose not. So were you a friend of Edwin's, then?"

She looked at me as though I were crazy.

"He left Juneau when he was *fifteen*. Now why would a thirteen-year-old girl spend time with a boy of fifteen? My father would have had a fit."

"Well, are there any anecdotes or stories you can tell me about the Pond family, or can you remember anything else that you think I might like to know?"

"That's about it. They were fond of pork chops. If you want to find out more, go to the Alaska State Library."

"I'll do that," I said. "Thanks for your help."

I was thrilled to meet the butcher's daughter, no matter how brusque and to-the-point she was. She had known my mother, and my uncle Edwin, and my grandparents! And they liked *pork chops!* My mother never told me that. It was a glorious feeling to be talking to someone who had known them so long ago. It amused me, however, that my nostalgic romanticism had gone right over her head. She must have concluded that the Pond/Hall genes were a little on the weird side, since they had produced an excitable, incomprehensibly exuberant specimen like myself, but the people of Juneau have different priorities when it comes to judging human nature. Good common sense, practicality, and a no-nonsense attitude are the qualities that work best when it comes to surviving the winter in Alaska.

"So, what did you find out about Percy Pond?" Gordon asked me, when I joined him at the brochure rack.

"Not much. He was partial to pork chops."

"What?"

I chuckled. "I'll explain later. Meanwhile we should go to the Alaska State Library now and do a little research."

"Well, that's not a bad idea. Not a bad idea at all. Let's get right over there. We only have six more hours in Juneau. We'd better not waste another minute."

Such is the nature of cruise ship travel.

CHAPTER FIVE

The Alaska State Library was on the 8th floor of the State Office Building, affectionately known as the S.O.B. It was located at 333 Willoughby Avenue in downtown Juneau, in an attractive white building set off by four two-storey columns, with wide stairs leading up to the front lobby. After making a few inquiries at the main desk, we were greeted by Sue Forsman, an administrator at the library. She was a friendly, intelligent, competent woman, and seemed to be happy to meet a close relative of Percy Pond's. I was relieved to see that not everyone in Juneau develops a tough, unsentimental attitude toward life.

"We've been longing to get some personal information about Percy Pond, but we didn't know where to find it," Sue told us. "It'll be interesting for us to get your perspective on him. The stories your mother and your grandmother handed down to you would be invaluable to us."

"Well, my mother told me lots of stories about him and her childhood in Juneau, so maybe I can be of some help."

"Excellent. How long will you be here?"

I looked at my watch. "Five hours and forty minutes."

"Good heavens! Is that all? Did you come in on one of the cruise ships?"

"Yes. The Sun Princess."

Sue nodded. "Well, can you stay for a while? I don't want to take up too much of your time. You'll want to see as much as you can while you're here in Juneau. But I'd love to talk to you long enough to get a quick sketch of what your grandfather was like as a person. I'd like to know about you and your family, too. We don't know what happened to his wife and children. It would be nice if you could fill me in on some of those things."

"You talk as though he were famous."

Sue looked at me carefully to see if I was joking. She seemed puzzled to see that I was not.

"Well, he *is* famous. His photographs are everywhere. They're in embassies and consulates all over the world. He took such sharp images that they've been enlarged to cover entire walls in our government buildings."

I stared at her.

"I'm sorry. I didn't know! My mother always told me that he was a talented photographer, but I had no idea he was really *that* good. I guess we always take it for granted that when people talk about their families, they exaggerate a bit. Sometimes more than a bit. But my mom never went so far as to tell me he was *famous!*"

"Well, maybe she didn't know. In fact, most of it was probably posthumous, although that's not necessarily true. He's buried in the pioneer section of Evergreen Cemetery, after all, which is quite an honor. So they must have known what an excellent photographer he was when he died."

Sue and I sat down together and had a cup of coffee while Gordon went for a stroll around the neighborhood.

"So what do you know about Percy Pond?" she asked me, leaning forward in anticipation. "Tell me anything you can remember."

I recounted everything I could think of, including his exciting romance with Hattie Hall, the Belle of the Ball. I also told her about how I had met my grandfather when he had visited us in Berkeley, California during the war.

"During the war?" Sue said, looking puzzled. "I thought you said a moment ago that you were born in England. Didn't you live in London during the war?"

"No. When the war broke out my mom and dad sent all of us to live with my grandmother, Harriet Hall, in Berkeley, California. They wanted us to be safe."

"All of you? How many were you?"

"There were three of us. My older sister, Sheila, my older brother, Craig, and me. The other three were born in England during the war. No, wait a minute. Actually, that's not quite so. Wilda and Nigel were born *during* the war, then Heather came along right afterwards."

"So you didn't see your parents the whole time the war was going on? Did you remember them at all?"

"No, I had no recollection of England before the war. I was only two when they sent us away."

"But the war lasted for five years! It must have seemed to you like you were meeting your parents for the first time when you were seven years old."

"Yes. That's exactly how it felt."

An image of the bizarre reunion came into my mind. When we got out of the car that day at the front steps of our house in London, a woman burst out of the door and kneeled down in front of me, enfolding me in her arms and weeping with joy. I allowed myself to be hugged, not knowing how to respond to this highly emotional stranger. I had looked forward to this moment for a long time, but now that it was happening I felt almost nothing. The nothingness surprised me, but I was relieved that my mother seemed so happy to see me. I had been worried that she wouldn't be all that thrilled to have me back home again.

But when I turned to go into the house, I looked up and saw *another* woman waiting by the door. I had never seen such a beautiful woman, nor had I ever seen such elegant clothes. She stood there smiling, looking like the Queen of England. I glanced back at the woman who had hugged me.

"Run, Sonia! Run!" she said. "Go quickly and hug your mother!"

I froze. That was my *mother?* The Queen of England? What was I supposed to *do?* And who was this *other* woman, then? Who was the woman who had hugged me? When I look back on it, it seems as though it all took place in slow motion. I moved toward the Queen, and she made a step toward me too, and eventually we came together in a sort of dream. I think she touched me, but I'm not sure. All I know is that she didn't hug me and she didn't kiss me, the way the other woman had. Why was *she* my mother, then? And who was the other woman? The one who had hugged me?

Sue didn't realize it, but she was getting close to the heart of something I didn't even want to think about. I had wounded my mother very deeply one day when I was in my teens, and the shame of it had never really been resolved. I accused her of sending me away because she didn't really love me or care about me, but of course that was the exact opposite of the truth. She had been faced with an extremely complicated choice, and she had undoubtedly made the most difficult decision of her entire life. She had been forced to determine whether to send her three children to safety far away, or to go with them and leave her husband behind to face the bombs alone.

All I knew at the time was that when Edwin had become desperately ill, my grandmother had taken her children to San Francisco and left her husband behind, and that was the last she had seen of him until he visited us in Berkeley that time, during the war. As for my mom, she never saw her dad again, and she had resented her mother bitterly for separating her from him. But when it looked as though the Germans were about to invade England, she found herself in the same position as her mother—faced with the need to separate her children from their parents and send them away for their own safety. Choices can be difficult, painful, permanent, and even fatal. The worst of it is we're often forced to make decisions on the spur of the moment, when we least expect it, with no time to deliberate or weigh the pros and cons. Then, to make matters worse, we have to live with the consequences for the rest of our lives.

"Well, let's get back to Percy Pond," Sue suggested, sensing, perhaps, that she had touched a nerve. "Tell me all about the impressions you had of him when he went to visit you in Berkeley during the war."

"He was by far and away the kindest, gentlest man I'd ever known," I said, without hesitation. "Nobody had ever treated me the way he did. He spent time with me, and read my books to me, and took walks with me, and asked me how I felt about things. He listened carefully to my little stories and all my senseless chatter. He was the first person who ever gave me the feeling I was somebody worth knowing. I couldn't have explained it at the time, but if Pinocchio's dream of becoming a real boy had come true, that would have perfectly described the way I felt when I was with my grandfather. I was no longer just a puppet to be seen and not heard—I was a real little girl."

"And how old were you then?"

"Five."

"Not to change the topic, but there's something else I wanted to ask you."

"Go ahead."

"Your grandfather spent a lot of time with the Tlingit tribe. I don't know if you know this, but he was so respected and loved by them that he was formally adopted by one of the families. I believe he was the first white man ever to receive such an honor."

"Really? That makes me feel proud. I knew he loved the first settlers and took many photographs of them, but I didn't know they had adopted him. It rounds him out a bit more in my own mind. They must have felt a great kinship with one another. I'd like to know the Tlingit tribe too, so I could get to know my grandfather better."

"You'll have to come back some day and live here for a while," Sue smiled. "But right now I'm curious to know if you have any idea why he and his partner, Lloyd Winter, were the only white men in those days who actually took the time to get to know them. To get to know them *well,* I mean. When a so-called Indian came down the street back then, most people would cross over to the other side. Everybody avoided the native inhabitants, or the "Indians" as they were called in your grandfather's day. People used to look down on them. Nobody wanted to have anything to do with them except your grandfather and Lloyd Winter. Why do you suppose that was?"

I thought about her question for a while. I was reminded of how he had once taken the time to talk to a five-year-old girl, endowing her with a feeling of valuable selfhood for the first time in her life. Perhaps he had done the same for the members of the Tlingit tribe, although it might very well have been the other way around. They had no doubt taught him a great deal that was of practical value to him when it came to surviving in the hinterland, and my guess was that he had learned some spiritual values from them as well. They were at ease with their simple, non-materialistic lives, and their hospitality and generosity must have touched him, especially since they had so little to give.

I was suddenly reminded of a little scrap of paper my mother had shown me one day, scribbled in Percy Pond's handwriting. Unfortunately I was unable to find it among her things after she died, but I did remember enough about it to locate the reference when the on-line search engines first made their appearance. It was from the March 17, 1911 issue of *The Spectator,* from an article written by Joseph Addison. I hadn't memorized the paragraph, so I couldn't recite it to Sue at that moment, but I believe it beautifully summarizes Percy Pond's philosophy of life:

> *True happiness is of a retired nature, and an enemy to pomp and noise. It arises, in the first place, from the enjoyment of one's self, and in the next from the friendship and conversation of a few select friends.*

After paraphrasing this for Sue, my mind went back to the things my mother used to tell me about the stories that

Percy had recounted to her about his father, who was born in Poland in 1843. His name was Louis Jaszynsky, and his family lived in a fairly substantial dwelling in Warsaw which was attacked by the Russians during one of their many incursions into Polish territory. According to my mother, a group of Russian Cossacks rode their horses right into the Jaszynsky residence and massacred everyone in sight—all except for the servants, who were not considered to be a military or political threat to the Russians. But Louis, who was only an infant at the time, was miraculously spared from a violent death at the hands of the soldiers. His wet nurse happened to be holding him under her shawl at the time the house was invaded, so the Russians were unaware of his existence and rode away to commit mayhem further on down the street.

After the dust settled the wet nurse gathered together her belongings and helped herself to the valuables left behind by the family and overlooked by the Russians, who were too busy killing people to think about looting and pillaging just then. She must have found enough money and valuables to book a passage for herself and baby Louis on a ship bound for America. So off they went, the wet nurse and her dead mistress's infant son, to reinvent themselves in a new and distant world across the sea.

According to my mother they eventually made their way to San Mateo, California. In 1870, when Louis Jaszynsky was 27, he married Marion Blanchard, and two years later their son Percy was born. In 1880 Louis died of unknown causes, and in 1883 his widow remarried a man by the name of E. S. Pond. Her new husband adopted her eleven-year-old son and gave him his name. So Percy Pond—a tall, blond youth who would not have existed if it hadn't been for the faithful wet nurse in his grandfather's employ—eventually grew up and married Harriet Hall in January, 1898.

What would the kindly wet nurse have said to Percy's father about human nature, the history of his forebears, and the meaning of life in general? She probably would have told him stories about Russian invasions and the destruction of Polish culture and civilization by a people who had the unmitigated gall to look down upon the inhabitants whose land they had willfully ravished.

How would Percy have been affected by these tales that were passed down to him by his father? Would he have remembered them after he married Hattie Hall and moved to Juneau? My guess was that he did, and he would not have wanted to side with the U.S. citizens who had the nerve to look down on the native peoples who had been living in Alaska long before their arrival. Not only had Percy's father perhaps educated him to this point of view, but Percy himself had a naturally kind heart and an instinct for empathizing with the victims of injustice. That dreamy, impractical, artistic nature of his was at it again.

I explained my hypothesis to Sue Forsman, who nodded thoughtfully.

"I think your story about your grandfather's Polish roots goes a long way toward explaining his attitude to the folks who got here first. It really is absurd how the people with power in this world automatically assume that this makes them superior in some way."

"They should read what Addison said about happiness."

Just then Gordon appeared in her office, accompanied by the woman from the front desk. She smiled and left us, eager to get back to her post.

"Your wife has been connecting quite a few dots for me here today," Sue told Gordon. "Our conversation has been very helpful. I can't begin to tell you how glad I am that you stopped by."

Before we left, Sue was kind enough to give me a copy of a book written by Victoria Wyatt, called *Images from the Inside Passage: An Alaskan Portrait by Winter and Pond*, which she had originally written as a PhD thesis. The book was filled with photographs taken by both my grandfather and Lloyd Winter. Nobody could have given me a gift that I could ever have cherished or appreciated more than Victoria Wyatt's book.

"Tell me something, Sue," I said, as we turned to go. "Where can we find my grandfather's studio, where he and Lloyd worked on their photos and sold curios?"

"Oh, that's a story in itself. Your grandfather and Lloyd Winter had a studio on Front Street, but there was a torrential rain one day and a huge mudslide washed down off Mount Juneau and pushed the whole building right to the other side of the street. There was nothing left of it after that."

"Good grief! What did they do?"

"Well, they eventually settled in another building on Main Street and put out their shingle again. But that was a long time ago, and the building is a tourist shop now. It's worth a visit, though. It would mean a lot to you personally."

"What happened to his photos? And his glass plates?"

"Oh, they just lay around in the other building, dusty and forgotten. But many years later, after your grandfather died, the plates were rescued by a friend who understood their enormous value. George Jorgenson was his name. So it's thanks to him that Winter and Pond are famous today. If it hadn't been for that man, nobody would have known who they were."

Once we were out on the street again, Gordon suddenly became my personal tourist guide in Juneau.

"I know where all the important stuff is now," he said proudly. "I cased the whole downtown area while you were in there talking with Sue."

He squired me all around town, showing me photos by Winter and Pond on display in various public places. We also found the tourist shop that Sue had told us about. It was a poignant moment for me when I stood there inside, trying to imagine being near Primrose as he worked on his photos. He would have made sure that they were well cropped and that the contrast was just right. I was glad I had once had my own darkroom and had some experience developing film and printing negatives. I never would have guessed back then that it would help me feel close to my grandfather one day.

After visiting some art galleries and museums, we ended up in the Evergreen Cemetery on Seater Street, where we found Percy Pond's grave at the far end, just where the trees start by the edge of Tongass National Forest. At first I was a bit disappointed by the modest appearance and positioning of his place of final rest, but on further reflection I concluded that it was entirely appropriate. Percy Pond was nothing if not self-effacing, and I'm sure he would have felt deeply satisfied to know he was resting close to the woods that led out to his beloved wilderness.

CHAPTER SIX

Our cruise to Alaska was over, and I felt the same way I always did at the end of a trip. I was ready to start out on a new adventure. I never wanted to go home. Not if it meant wrangling with head office buyers or keeping an eye on plant workers who never seemed to realize that I could clearly hear them say, "Watch out, here she comes!" whenever they saw me approaching.

We were holed up now in The Delta Vancouver Airport Hotel on the banks of the Fraser River. Gordon was at the window, staring out at the marina and looking rather wistful.

"I see nautical longings reflected deep in your eyes," I said to him, hoping to stir him up into a frenzy of wanderlust matched only by my own.

"Nah. I was just counting the raindrops. Why does it always rain in Vancouver? Don't they every get tired of it?"

"Why don't we just charter a boat and sail to Hawaii?"

"Right. You'd be heaving over the side, just when I needed you most."

"Okay, so let's stick to airplanes, then. Let's just swing by San Francisco on our way home. What do you say?"

"What's in San Francisco?"

"16 Divisadero Street."

"What's that supposed to mean?"

"My mom used to live at 16 Divisadero Street. Her mother took her there with her brother Edwin when he got heart trouble and had to leave Alaska."

"Oh."

"We're here on the West Coast now. We'd save a lot of money if we went to San Francisco from here, rather than coming all the way back from Nova Scotia to see her house."

"You think I don't notice that you're blatantly appealing to my parsimonious nature?"

"Why, whatever makes you say that?" I asked, trying to look innocent. "Actually, I was appealing to your sense of efficiency. *You're* the efficiency expert, not me."

My grandmother's house at 16 Divisadero Street had seen better days. It was a long, narrow, unprepossessing dwelling sandwiched between two other buildings on a rather dreary street that lacked an adequate number of trees. The rest of the neighborhood didn't look particularly inviting either, but it might have gone downhill since my grandmother had lived there. It struck me as rather depressing that the Belle of the Ball at San Francisco's Winter Cotillion had ended up in such "straitened circumstances," as she used to describe her financial situation in Juneau.

I remember my mother saying that in her day husbands were expected to support their wives. Once a young woman was married, her father washed his hands of her completely. It would have been profoundly embarrassing to any husband if he'd had to depend on friends or in-laws for financial aid. Things are quite different nowadays, but this attitude might explain my grandmother's impatience with Primrose for not being a particularly successful bread winner.

Her frustration with her husband's efforts was probably born of the mortal fear that she and her children might end up in the poorhouse, a terrifying fate to which she often used to refer. But Hattie Hall was a fighter and a survivor, and she was not going to allow the poorhouse to intimidate her or become a looming presence in her life. She marched right out the door of her house one day and applied for a position as a teacher at a private school for young ladies in San Francisco. Not only did she get the job, but she ended up becoming the principal of the school. So much for the money problems.

"Gordon, do you think I should ring the bell?"

"No, heavens no!" he said, looking alarmed. "There's no need to disturb anyone. The house doesn't mean anything to you. You never lived here, after all."

"So why did we come to San Francisco, then?" I asked him.

"San Francisco's one of the most beautiful cities I know. There's a lot to see and do here. And don't forget the rest of the Bay Area. We could visit the campus at the University of California at Berkeley where you did your graduate work for your M.A., or you could show me around San Francisco State College, where you used to teach."

"They call it San Francisco State University now. But you're right. I'd love to show you those places."

"We can have lunch at Fisherman's Wharf, overlooking San Francisco Bay," he went on. "We'll have fresh fish and a Mediterranean salad and then we'll go get some chocolates from Ghirardelli Square."

Gordon sure knew how to tempt a girl.

"Okay, but let's take a quick peek at Buena Vista Park first. It's only a couple of blocks away. My mother used to talk about how she'd go there with her friends. I'd like to walk where she walked, you know what I mean? I promise I won't put you through any agony. No *real* agony anyway," I added, when I saw the skeptical look on his face.

The "quick peek" at Buena Vista Park turned out to be a hike that took all morning, but it was eminently worthwhile. The grounds were laid out on a steep slope leading up to a small lawn at the very peak. From there we were able to get a beautiful view to the east, north, and west, including the Golden Gate Bridge and the Marin Headlands. We met a hiker up there who recommended that we go down to "The Window," located on the west side of the slope. It turned out to be a lookout that showed us another spectacular view, this time of Golden Gate Park and the Pacific Ocean.

"I'll bet my mom was happy here in this park," I said dreamily. "I don't see how she couldn't have been. A view like this makes your spirit soar, like a good operatic aria. Too bad we can't be listening to Pavarotti right now."

"Yeah, too bad," said Gordon, sarcastically.

"Hey, I just thought of something. You want to know what *divisadero* means?"

"Do I have a choice?"

"It means *vantage point* in Spanish."

"Vantage point," Gordon mused. "That's interesting."

"Yes. It comes from the verb *divisar*, which means *to discern*. In other words, it refers to some sort of a high place where you can get a good view of the surrounding terrain. A vantage point is like a viewpoint, right? Hikers are always looking for high spots so they can figure out what path they should take. That's what we're doing here in San Francisco. Buena Vista Park has answered my question. *Buena Vista* means *beautiful view*, of course. So I'm looking for a lovely view with a vantage point that will help me develop a solid understanding of the existential questions I've never been able to come to grips with before. How do you like that?"

"There you go!" Gordon smiled. "16 Divisadero Street and Buena Vista Park are the keys to the meaning of life!"

"You got it!" I said, throwing grass at him and gleefully chasing him down the hill.

As I lay in bed that night I thought about the house on Divisadero Street where my grandmother had nursed Edwin for seventeen years, until his heart had finally stopped when he reached the age of thirty-two. Those were seventeen years he probably never would have enjoyed if she hadn't moved him to San Francisco and taken care of him there. But how many of those seventeen years had been stolen from my mother's life? She used to tell me how my grandmother hovered incessantly over Edwin, worried about anything that could possibly affect his heart, while my mom wistfully watched this *danse macabre* from the sidelines.

My mother felt jealous of the attention my grandmother lavished on my uncle Edwin, but she always felt guilty about her jealousy, and did her best to cover it up. It wouldn't have been so bad, she used to say, if Edwin hadn't been such a brat. He would tease her and get her into trouble, just to see her squirm. I imagine he had his own issues with jealousy when she came home from a nice long hike with her friends in Buena Vista Park, a place where he was strictly forbidden to go lest he exert himself by climbing the hill. They hotly resented each other, those two kids, and my grandmother probably felt quite frazzled by having to hold down a full-time position as a teacher as well as another demanding job as Edwin's caregiver. She had no patience for complaints and arguments and unnecessary tensions, so my mother learned to be the peacekeeper.

On top of all this, my mom missed Primrose so much it almost made her sick with sorrow and yearning. She had been his special little girl, and now he was gone forever. She secretly blamed her mother for leaving him in the lurch, but she never said anything about how she felt. How could she? She knew with her head that her mother had made the right decision as far as Edwin's health was concerned, but in her heart she felt that her mother had harmed her as much as she had helped Edwin when she had made the decision to leave Alaska. Her heart had been broken by this separation. Does a physical heart matter more than the heart that houses all the love and the pain and the hopes and desires of a person's whole being?

My grandmother expected her to be helpful around the house and be a cheerful, uncomplaining companion to ease the difficult burden of her own fears and disappointments. My mom was just a teenager in those days, but she had the strength of character to get through her adolescence without creating any major trouble for anyone else. Whether this also applied to herself is, of course, a moot point. Any young person in her situation would have had problems. Maybe one of my mom's biggest trials was that she had nobody to turn to for help or advice or consolation. At least, she never spoke to me about any such person.

Her life took a turn for the better in 1921 when she was accepted as an undergraduate at the University of California at Berkeley. True to her habit in the days when she and Edwin were in Juneau, she soon devised nicknames for all her college "chums," as she called them in the letters she used to send me when I was also a student there.

Have you seen Mrs. Low-Beer yet? Yes, that's really her name, hard as it may be to believe. If you've lost that telephone number I left on the phone table, do contact her through the Faculty Club. It needn't be more than one lunch with "the Bit." Strange characters are in the offing: "the Bit," "the Wisp," and "the Orchid." They were all chums of mine when we were at college together, and they might have some interesting contacts that could lead in the direction of a nice young man. Who knows?

Naturally I was a very independent, opinionated young woman in those days, and I didn't want my mother's old chums to introduce me to any "nice young men." She evidently foresaw my neglectful attitude when it came to making contact with her friends, so a few weeks later she gently reminded me that I might find them interesting. When I look back on it now, I realize that I would have been fortunate indeed if *they* had found *me* to be mildly interesting in some way.

I know you'd like "The Bit" very much. She was way ahead of her contemporaries in intellect, vocabulary, and general knowledge, but it didn't prevent us from having fun, jolly laughter, and rollicking adventures together. Her voice has gone down an octave, and she may be old-looking now, but as a girl she resembled you in appearance, and if you were to have lunch with her you wouldn't be bored. I left you her address, which you've probably lost, so leave a note at the Faculty Club, and if you do see her, please write me every detail!

My mother, who had worked so hard to put me in touch with old chums who could lead me in the general direction of a presentable young man, was herself led quite by accident (35 years before she sent me the letter copied above) to the man who would eventually become her husband. Nobody had made even the slightest attempt to lead her in the right direction, nor had it occurred to anyone to appeal to people with connections. My mother had been left entirely to her own devices, and was quite content to spend most of her time with the "Bit," the "Wisp," and the "Orchid."

It all began one day when Edwin, who by this time had become a noteworthy figure in San Francisco commercial art circles, was preparing to receive a new client.

"I don't want *you* hanging around when he gets here," he said to my mom. "This man is an important businessman, and I want to make a good impression on him. I want him to see me as a serious, professional artist, and I can't bring it off if my kid sister is puttering around in the background."

"Oh, drop dead," my mom said irritably, then quickly bit her tongue.

"Get lost, will you?" he shot back.

After an unsuccessful attempt to get in touch with her chums, my mother put on her coat and set off for Buena Vista Park. She stayed there for the entire afternoon, reading library books and preparing for her classes the next day. I wouldn't be surprised if she thought rather bitterly about how to discern the best way to handle her annoying brother. Maybe she thought that she would enjoy a better vantage point from the heights of Buena Vista Park. Be that as it may, at sunset she gathered up her books and headed home, feeling certain that by then Edwin's precious gentleman caller would have concluded his business and gone away.

When she came through the doorway she was surprised to see the dinner table set for four, with her mother leaning over to place the last serving dish on the runner. She cast my mom a sideward glance, as much as to say, "Where were *you* when I needed you to help me in the kitchen?"

Instead she said, "Hello Marion Belle, dear. I'd like you to meet Mr. Harrison. He's a business client of Edwin's, and I've asked him to stay for dinner."

Mr. Harrison got up from the armchair and extended his hand to my mother, who blushed crimson and shot a nervous look at Edwin. She knew he didn't appreciate having her around when he was trying to impress a client, but there was nothing she could do. They had invited him to dinner, and she was, after all, a member of the family.

"How do you do, Miss Pond," he said, delicately taking her hand in his own.

"I'm pleased to meet you, Mr. Harrison," my mother replied demurely, looking down at her feet.

"Your brother has told me a great deal about you, and I was impressed with what he said. He tells me that you're a very good artist, too. The gift must run in the family."

"My brother isn't always very truthful," my mother said, managing to take a pot shot at Edwin while at the same time appearing to be appropriately modest.

The dinner party went particularly well, thanks mainly to Mr. Harrison's unusually clever wit and vivid stories. He also had the gift of listening with ardent interest to whatever his hostess happened to be saying. He acted as though she were the most fascinating, amusing woman he had ever met, and before the dinner was over he had the Belle of the Ball eating out of the palm of his hand. My grandmother was perhaps a bit too vain and easily flattered to realize what was happening. She accepted his admiring comments at face value, without realizing that he was sophisticated enough to know that the best way to court a beautiful young woman was to win over her mother first.

My grandmother's vanity and her eye-fluttering attitude toward the handsome, successful, urbane, witty Mr. Harrison almost put an end to the courtship before it even began.

I should let my mom speak for herself:

Granny was a truly marvelous teacher, and still remembered! She was much better at handling impersonal relationships, though. In other words, she was better with a class than she was with her own family. When I became a teenager she was convinced that I had made up my mind to challenge her supremacy (a thing I never would have even <u>attempted</u> to do in any way, shape, or form!), so I was cloistered away and watched like a hawk. But when beaux actually did come calling, I became a deadly rival—she treated them as if they were <u>her</u> beaux! There was one in particular that she was determined to have me marry. When I refused him she was furious and said he was the best beau <u>I'd</u> ever have, since I wasn't capable of attracting anyone as good as he was again.

Then along came Daddy, and he was even <u>better</u> than the first one, so she put a great deal of effort into getting me to agree. As you know, this nearly upset the applecart. And it would have, too, if Daddy hadn't been so determined.

Determination was without a doubt one of my father's most outstanding qualities. He threw himself into everything he did with a resolve and a sense of purpose that made him hard to beat on any battle front. When it came to women, all they had to do was act hard to get and he would pursue them until they began to tire, then he'd land them with a flying tackle. Some women loved to be pursued with such ardent tenacity. It meant dining out, expensive gifts, adventurous trips, exciting night clubs, and envious female competitors.

But if women had seen him only from that perspective, their view of him would have been too limited. He was more complicated than that. Far from being an ordinary Don Juan or a two-dimensional libertine who responded automatically to the scent of the hard-to-get woman, Kay Harrison was a highly intelligent, passionate, complex man with a troubled heart and genuine sensitivities. He was capable of suffering deeply. He had a great appreciation for art and literature. When he loved, he loved for many of the right reasons, and yearned to share the universe with a true soul mate. He was a romantic, yes, but not a shoddy one. He'd have sacrificed his life for the woman he loved at the moment, and he would have gone to any length to lay the world at her feet.

The only problem with being a true romantic is that you can never hope to marry the woman of your dreams. As soon as she is tied down and has nowhere to run, then it's game over. My father had once been married to a talented New York artist, but after a few months of marriage the princess he had conjured up in his mind turned into a toad. Not just an ordinary, garden variety toad. She was a colorful, artistic, humorous one, but a toad nonetheless. The interesting thing is that she felt exactly the same way about him, so they had a marvelous time laughing about it and talking it all over, and in the end they parted on the very best of terms.

Now here was Marion Belle Pond—a smart, beautiful, shy and sensitive woman who was clearly more than capable of understanding and appreciating his complicated nature and his romantic personality. She was obviously good at getting along well with difficult people, judging from the fact that she was still living in the same household as her domineering mother and her spoiled, ailing brother. The most interesting and challenging thing about her, however, was that she was just as determined *not* to marry Kay Harrison as he was hell bent on getting her to change her mind. But what, he wondered, was making her hesitate? If he could get to the bottom of it, he would surely be able to figure out a strategy for winning this charming, delectable battle-to-be. It would just be a matter of time before he made Marion Belle Pond his bride-to-be.

The trouble with this modest woman was that she wasn't playing a game. She wasn't playing hard to get, she *was* hard to get. She wasn't just playing the role of an old-fashioned Southern Belle, she was *Marion* Belle—an individual in her own right. What my father failed to realize at the time, and which largely accounted for my mother's reluctance to allow herself to be courted by him, was that she instinctively knew he would have a hard time honoring any vow that required him to be faithful. She had taken note of many things about Kay Harrison at the dinner table that night, and most of them had impressed her favorably. But as she had listened to his intriguing stories and witty comments about life and human nature, it dawned on her that this was a man with a roving eye, and for Marion Belle that was a deal breaker.

After my father went home that night, Edwin pulled my mother aside and warned her not to hitch her wagon to this man's star, or she would live to regret it. He had also seen something in him that made him doubt that he would ever be good husband material. My mother was actually quite moved by her brother's genuine concern for her well-being. In spite of his many irritating faults and his endless barbs, he was, underneath it all, a decent human being. My mom always remembered his words of warning with gratitude, and she listened to them in much the same way as Ophelia listened to the words of her own brother in *Hamlet,* Act I, Scene III:

> *I shall the effect of this good lesson keep,*
> *As watchman to my heart. But, good my brother,*
> *Do not, as some ungracious pastors do,*
> *Show me the steep and thorny way to heaven;*
> *Whiles, like a puff'd and reckless libertine,*
> *Himself the primrose path of dalliance treads,*
> *And recks not his own rede.*

But in spite of all her best efforts to be a good watchman to her heart, my mother finally succumbed to the romantic

Kay Harrison. What won her over, however, was not the fact that he squired her around town in high style or that he showered her with expensive gifts from exotic lands. That would have made him no more exciting to her than Frank Sinatra's callow, party-animal character in *The Tender Trap.* No, she felt he was more like Trevor Howard's brooding, sensitive character in *Brief Encounter,* with some touches of Laurence Olivier's Heathcliff adding mystery, pride, and danger to the mix. Mr. Harrison had the irresistible spirit of a man who dared to live his life without a lightning rod, and who was not afraid of being struck by a *coup de foudre* sent down by the gods on Mount Olympus. Life with such a man would never be dull.

The Belle of the Ball had found a new beau, even if she did have to share him reluctantly with her own daughter. My mother, however, was too principled a woman to tread the primrose path of dalliance lightly, but she was also aware that life could be unspeakably boring sometimes. Only the most dyed-in-the-wool prude would hesitate to spice it up with a little pinch of dalliance.

CHAPTER SEVEN

It was just another sunny day in San Francisco, like so many others that followed one after the other. My mom recounted to me how the Pond family had been sitting around the dining room table that day, stuffing envelopes with elegant wedding invitations.

"Say," said Edwin, looking up from his work. "Guess who's on *my* list?"

"Who?" my mother asked, just to be nice.

"Your secret admirer," Edwin said, with a snicker.

"I don't have any secret admirers."

"Yes, you do."

"Do not."

"Oh, *hush*, you two," my grandmother said impatiently. "You sound like a couple of schoolchildren."

My mother frowned. It was just like Edwin to goad her into responding with indignation to one of his disparaging remarks, only to have their mother step in and tell them *both* to stop their quarreling and behave like adults. It was no use ignoring him, either. He would simply keep it up until she eventually responded, and that's when she'd hear "Oh *hush*, you two," while Edwin chuckled softly into his hand. Edwin Triumphant, the boy who never grew up.

"Who are you writing to now?" my grandmother asked, leaning over to look at Edwin's envelope.

He had even managed to goad *her* into succumbing to her curiosity, my mother thought, her irritation rising again.

Edwin playfully covered the envelope with his hands, leaning over it so she couldn't see it or snatch it away.

"Show it to me!" my grandmother squealed, as though Edwin's shenanigans were the most amusing events of the day.

"No!"

"Edwin, give me that, you naughty boy!"

He leaped up from his chair and made straight for the kitchen, waving the envelope over his head. My grandmother went suddenly pale.

"Edwin, don't exert yourself," she cried, jumping up and following him. "Don't get too excited! Remember what the doctor said. You have to stay calm! Your heart!"

"Yes, I know all about my heart," he laughed. "But does my heart know *me*? That's the real question. Does anyone know either me or my heart? Do they *care?*"

"Edwin, sit down and I'll get you some bread and butter and jam, and a nice hot pot of weak tea. It's time for a snack, anyway. Now be a good boy and show me the envelope. If Marion Belle has secret admirers, we'll have to warn Kay."

It was all a game with those two, my mother thought. Edwin would tease her and worry her, and she would think he was her dear, delightful boy. When would they ever get tired of the same old nonsense? She knew, though, that the games were just a way of expressing their love and affection, and my mom, as usual, began to feel ashamed of her jealousy and for being so resentful of a young man who was dying.

She was glad she'd soon be getting married and moving away. It wouldn't be soon enough, though, as far as she was concerned. Then she suddenly felt worried. She had to be honest with herself. Was she marrying Kay just to get out of the house? Would she pay some terrible price for making a precipitous, ill-advised decision? Which was worse, a galling present or an unknown future? Maybe she was exaggerating the level of irritation she had been dealing with for so long. She told herself sternly to stop feeling sorry for herself and have a little more gratitude for her blessings. She made a determined effort to focus on all the good things in her life, starting with her upcoming nuptials. Kay had been incredibly kind and generous about it all. He had booked the banquet hall at the St. Francis Hotel for February 5th, 1927, and had made all the arrangements for the caterers. He had even seen to such details as getting the marriage license and finding an Episcopalian minister to perform the ceremony. In fact, he had taken care of everything as though it were something he did every day. No fuss, no bother. Everything was so easy when my father was in charge. The only thing Mom had had to do for herself was pick out a wedding dress, and even then my dad had gallantly footed the bill. The only other thing he had allowed the rest of the Ponds to do for themselves was to send out the wedding invitations. They had all agreed that their friends should receive personalized cards.

My mom knew that the invitation that Edwin had been writing to her so-called "secret admirer" was now sitting unnoticed on top of the ice box. She decided to go quietly into the kitchen while nobody was looking and check out the addressee.

"Good for you, Marion Belle," my grandmother called after her. "I was wondering when you were going to put the kettle on."

My mother frowned. Who was she, Cinderella? She immediately told herself to button her lips. She'd maintain strict silence. She would not complain, not even under her breath. Soon she would be Mrs. Kay Harrison, and nothing would ever be the same again. The last thing she wanted to do was create hurt feelings and regrets in the few remaining weeks of her tenure as the Perpetual Caregiver. She had given these two people everything she had. Now maybe she would be allowed to take a little bit from the generous-hearted Kay Harrison.

She loved him for not being parsimonious. She loved him for believing that she was a woman worthy of sharing his life with him. She loved him for his fearless, optimistic view of the future and their place in it together.

"What are you up to, Marion Belle?" my grandmother called out. "Did you put the kettle on?"

"Yes, yes. I'm doing it," my mom said, shaking herself out of her reverie.

While she waited for the water to boil, she snatched the envelope off the ice box and quickly read the address.

Mr. Paul Preston
San Francisco Veterans' Medical Center
Psychiatric Ward
4150 Clement Street
San Francisco, California

Years later my mother told me that when she saw Paul's name associated with a psychiatric ward, she had felt such a profound and electrifying shock go through her that she thought for a moment she was going to faint. Paul Preston, the epitome of the tall, dark, and handsome figure of every young girl's dreams; Paul, who could have been Rudolph Valentino's brother but who had never wanted to capitalize on his good looks; Paul, her brother's friend and former tutor... this legendary Paul Preston had ended up in a psychiatric ward!

My mother sat down heavily on the kitchen stool and began to think. Why hadn't Edwin told her that Paul was in a psychiatric ward? Why wasn't Edwin more deeply moved by his former tutor's fate? How could he joke around while he held Paul's wedding invitation in his hand? Why and how could this have happened to Paul?

My mom knew only one thing that could explain it. He had fought in the Great War, and he must have gone through some dreadful experience or experiences on the battlefield. He had not been physically wounded himself, but he must have seen terrible things that had left him deeply wounded in his heart and soul. He had seemed all right, though, when he was Edwin's tutor just after the war. He had been around for quite a while after that, visiting Edwin and having dinner with the family, and chatting about his plans and dreams. Then one day he had mysteriously disappeared, and my mom had never seen him again. She sensed that he might have had feelings for her, but she didn't believe there was any reason for her to be the cause of his decision to bow out of their lives like that. She had always thought it was strange that he simply upped and left without a word of explanation, but she trusted that he had his reasons, and she had left it at that.

"What are you sitting there looking so mournful about?" my grandmother asked, appearing suddenly in front of my mother. "You have nothing to be sad about. You're going to marry the best beau you've ever had or are ever likely to have. You should rejoice and be happy."

"Do you know why Paul is in a psychiatric ward?" my mom blurted out.

My grandmother just stood there, looking thunderstruck.

"Who told you that?" she asked finally.

"I saw it on his wedding invitation."

My grandmother looked over at Edwin, who shrugged.

"Go ahead and tell her, Ma," he said. "She was bound to find out sooner or later."

My grandmother looked speculatively at my mother for a moment or two, then finally decided to speak.

"He suffered from shell shock as a result of the war. He saw some awful things, but he wasn't the sort of person who could get over it. He brooded on it, and allowed it to take root in his soul. He couldn't shake it off, and none of us could help him, since we didn't share the same experiences. He tried to explain, and we tried to listen, but nothing much ever came of his efforts to communicate his feelings. I'm sure he felt discouraged."

"Where was *I* all this time?" my mom wanted to know.

"Where were you? You were at college. Where do you think you were?"

"But I came home every night."

"Yes, well Paul always went home before you got back for dinner. Remember? He didn't like to walk in the dark, so he'd leave in the afternoon. He said when it was dark he could see the bombs and the mortar fire all around him. It made him queasy. It was just one of the many phobias he'd developed."

My mother was distressed to hear what had become of Paul Preston. He was too lovely a man to have been hurt that way, she told me many years later. He had had such promise, so much to contribute, such hope for a better, more beautiful world. It seemed to her that the best people always suffered the most in this life.

My mother's and father's wedding was a glorious affair, and one that would long be remembered by the social set. All of San Francisco was there, for the Belle of the Ball had kept up her contacts, and being the head mistress of a well-regarded private girls' school was enough to win over the people who didn't remember her from before she had moved to Alaska.

My mother was only sorry that Primrose wasn't there. She was secretly hoping that he would show up unannounced in order to surprise her, but this had turned out to be only wishful thinking on her part. So Edwin had given her away, while my grandmother watched his every move to make sure he did nothing to strain his heart.

My father was a great hit with the wedding guests. He entertained everyone with his wit and consummate skill as a story teller, but he also delighted the guests with his listening abilities, too. When he wanted to he could make people feel important and bigger than life, but woe betide the individuals who felt *self*-important in his presence, or who looked down on him or his chosen friends—he wouldn't hesitate to fell them with his sharp tongue. But nothing like that happened on his wedding day. He was on his very best behavior on that bright, auspicious and memorable occasion, and a first-class time was had by all.

While the guests were laughing and talking and enjoying themselves, one particular individual had been observing the celebration from the shadows at the rear of the magnificent banquet hall. He was a tall, dark, and handsome man, who could easily have been mistaken for Rudolph Valentino. When all the speeches had been made, when all the glasses had been clinked, and when all the wishes for a long and happy life had been duly expressed, Paul Preston stepped forward and faced the throng of smiling guests. He picked up the nearest mike and tapped it sharply two or three times and cleared his throat.

"I'm a friend of the bride's," he began, in a deep and hollow voice. "I've known Marion Belle since the day she was born in Juneau, Alaska, on November 7th, 1904."

All heads turned to look at the blushing bride, who was indeed blushing at that moment with the embarrassment of having had her exact age revealed to one and all.

"Marion Belle is not only a princess among princesses," he went on, "she is an angel among angels. When I was on the battlefield and men were dying all around me, it was her image that led me through the horrors of that carnage. It was the thought of her that saved me from losing all faith in this world when I witnessed with my own eyes the reality of man's inhumanity to man."

People rustled uncomfortably in their starched shirts and stiffly-layered skirts, uncertain at that point if they should feel moved by this man's battlefield experiences or disturbed by the gory battle scenes and his unembarrassed description of Kay Harrison's new bride. It was all rather inappropriate, they felt, for him to be talking with such euphoric rapture about the angel in their midst.

"I didn't come away from the war unaffected by the horrors of the battlefield," Paul continued. "The ground was soaked with blood. There were severed limbs as far as the eye could see. Men were tripping on them, and slipping on the blood…"

Just then my father rose to his feet and walked over to Paul, whom he had never met and for whom my mother had not yet had a chance to prepare him. The faces of the guests, by that time, had turned chalk white. They fully expected my father to take away his microphone and to usher him firmly but gently right out the door. Instead, he put his left arm around Paul's shoulders and picked up a second mike with his right hand.

"My friend here is a poet," he said, looking at Paul with undisguised admiration. "And as you all know, poets always tell the truth. For without truth, how could we possibly even *begin* to understand the meaning of life? It's the métier and the duty of all poets to clear the way to a better and deeper appreciation of our small but violently colorful planet, lost as it is in a galaxy of stars that wait expectantly for us, yes *us,* to shed light on their purpose in the firmament.

"My friend has grasped this truth in all its multi-faceted beauty. He also knows that nothing can be accomplished without the help of God and all his angels, and this is what he came here to tell you today. For any wedding is a new beginning, a joining of two people who will be adding new stars to the universe. The profound honor of our calling to be human beings on our unique and alarming little planet is well nigh indescribable, and that's why we need poets to interpret its meaning for our general enlightenment."

Nobody at the wedding that day had the faintest idea what my father had just said, but it sounded profound and it had certainly been effective in saving a situation that had been about to deteriorate into something rather embarrassing from any point of view.

"And so I thank you, my friend," my father said, turning to smile at Paul's composed and glowing face. "I invite you to join us at the head table, where you can get a close-up view of the face of your special angel before I gather her up in my arms and carry her up the gangplank of our slow boat to Japan. I promise to take very good care of her for you."

There was a dead silence in the banquet hall as my father gently showed Paul to his place of honor at the head table. Then suddenly all the guests began to applaud. Two or three of them got to their feet, then everybody rose and gave Paul Preston and Kay Harrison a standing ovation.

My mother was looking at her new husband with an expression of genuine, heart-felt adoration. She always told me that she never really fell properly in love with my dad until their wedding day. It was a love that provided her with the strength to stand by him in sickness and in health, for better or for worse, from that day forward, until death finally parted them.

There would be good times and bad times, of course, as there are in any marriage, but what helped my mom over the bad times more than anything else was the memory of my dad's gallant, sensitive treatment of a suffering human being who desperately needed to be accepted and understood, as well as honored and reassured. When my dad's eyes began their inevitable roving, my mother always remembered him as he had been on their wedding day. It was the day when the seeds of unconditional love first took root in her heart.

Just then the orchestra started playing. My dad jumped up and invited my mother to dance. They were a handsome couple, and they danced with the confidence of a man and woman who were well practiced in the art.

"It was all because Daddy was such a good leader," my mom would say later. "He was blessed with supreme self-confidence, and it rubbed off on me, too. When I was with him I felt that together we could accomplish anything we set our minds to. It was the most marvelous feeling. I thought I was walking on air."

Mr. and Mrs. Kay Harrison were the first to take their leave that night. They bid their guests farewell and asked them to enjoy themselves, to drink hearty, and to dance the night away. They, meanwhile, had a ship to catch.

"Goodbye, Marion Belle," said the *Wisp.*

"Say hello to Tokyo for me," the *Orchid* chimed in.

"Bring us back some kimonos," the *Bit* reminded her.

There were tears and laughter and promises and hugs and kisses all around, then the newlyweds made their escape amid showers of confetti and good wishes for a successful new venture start-up in Japan.

My mother turned around again just before they left the banquet hall. She had forgotten to say goodbye to Paul, and she wanted to go back and find him. But she needn't have worried. There he stood, tall and handsome in the front row of the well-wishers, looking like his old self. He gave my mom a broad grin and waved his hand. Then he winked and nodded at my dad, and gave him a thumbs-up.

CHAPTER EIGHT

For old time's sake, Gordon and I decided to stay in the St. Francis Hotel in San Francisco. The year was 1998, exactly 71 years after the wedding of Kay Harrison and Marion Belle Pond had taken place in the banquet hall. It was still there, that banquet hall, looking much the same, I supposed, as it had back in those days. There had probably been multiple renovations since the day my parents were married, but I had the feeling that if my mother had been there at the St. Francis with Gordon and me that morning, she would have been delighted to see the banquet hall still looking much the way it did in 1927.

"I had a good time yesterday," Gordon said, casually munching a croissant. "I liked seeing your mother's house at 16 Divisadero Street. Your grandmother's house, I mean."

"It belonged to my *great* grandparents, actually."

"Your great grandparents, then," he said, taking another sip of his black coffee.

Gordon had been drinking black coffee ever since I'd met him four decades before. I still didn't know how he could stand drinking his coffee black. I had never been able to gag down anything that bitter. Surely most normal people had to hold their noses and *learn* to swallow bitter things like black coffee and dark chocolate. Weren't we all hard-wired from back in the caveman days to avoid poison, and isn't poison always bitter? I didn't know for sure. I'm not really a connoisseur of the flavor of poison.

"So where would you like to go today?" Gordon asked. "How about visiting the house in Berkeley, where you lived with your grandmother during the war?"

"Okay then," I said.

"So do you know where it is, the house in Berkeley?"

"46 Domingo Avenue."

"Whoa! That's pretty impressive."

"What is?"

"Telling me the address right off the bat like that."

"Oh, I don't know. Don't most people remember where they grew up? What was *your* address, for example?"

"12 Martense Street, in Brooklyn, New York. It was in Flatbush."

"There you go. See?"

"I guess you're right. So what do you say? Shall we go to… where was it again?"

"46 Domingo Avenue."

"Right. Do you want to show me your old house? Hey, wait a minute. What happened to your grandmother's house at 16 Divisadero Street? Why did she move to Berkeley?"

"She sold the house and went to England to live with my parents after Edwin died. It was in the mid 1930's, but I don't really know what year it was when she actually sold the house. Anyway, my parents were back from Japan, and they'd bought a townhouse in Mayfair. So my grandmother moved in with them and we all lived there together. My mom and dad, Granny, Josy, Sheila, Craig, and me."

"Josy? Who was she?"

"Our nanny and our housekeeper."

"Oh, okay. But wait a minute. How can you remember that? You left London when you were only two."

"You're right. So I don't recall anything from before the war. I just know what the others told me."

"Your first memories were of the house in Berkeley?"

"Right. When we lived at 46 Domingo Avenue."

"Domingo. That means *Sunday,* doesn't it?"

"Good for you, Gordon! How'd you know that?"

"Oh, I don't tell you everything. I know a little Spanish. I just don't like to use it in front of *you.*"

"Hah. You're afraid I'll correct you?"

"No. I'm afraid you'll laugh."

As we drove toward Berkeley I was surprised to find that I wasn't really looking forward to visiting our old house there. Our lives in Berkeley during the war had not been outstandingly happy. First of all, my grandmother was not at all pleased at the prospect of moving out of the comfortable townhouse at 49 Charles Street in London, where my father had made it possible for her to live like a *grande dame*. Not only did Josy keep us children from making a nuisance of ourselves, but there was a housemaid and a chauffeur to cater to any other whim that happened to strike my grandmother's fancy. She was the queen bee, and she gloried in having attained her rightful place in the world at last.

But it was a moment of glory that turned out to be very short-lived, for just as she was beginning to hit her stride, along came Hitler and put the kibosh on it. On September 3, 1939, England declared war on Germany. By early 1940, the British suspected that there was a real possibility that Hitler would cross the English Channel and invade their country, so families began exploring ways of sending their children to places of relative safety. Many were sent to friends and family in rural areas, and others were shipped off to Canada and the United States.

So my father booked passage on the *George Washington* for my grandmother, Sheila, Craig and me, and off we went to America. I have no recollection of this voyage, but I was told that I was highly dissatisfied with the accommodations, and demanded often and loudly to be taken to the garden. Nobody had any idea what to make of this peculiar request, considering we were in the middle of the Atlantic Ocean, so it went largely ignored. In retrospect, though, I imagine that in my two-year-old mind it had occurred to me that if someone would be kind enough to take me to the tiny garden behind the townhouse on Charles Street, I would easily be able to find my way back indoors from there. All I know is that I, along with most of the other little children on board, wanted more than anything else to be home again on *terra firma*, nestled in our mothers' arms.

We ended up in Berkeley, where my father had rented the house at 46 Domingo Avenue. My grandmother was not in the least bit happy to find herself the sole proprietor of three children. She had been there and done that, and she was clearly not looking forward to starting the job all over again, especially now that she was sixty-seven years old, an age that in those days was universally described as "elderly."

To top it all off, we kids were the fruit of Marion Belle's disobedience. My grandmother had warned her not to have more than one child, or two at the very most, for she was clearly not able to take care of any more than that. Granny was of the unshakable opinion that my mother's perceived incompetence was directly inherited from Percy Pond, that absurdly impractical dreamer. It seemed quite obvious to my grandmother that she would be an utter failure at raising children, who all needed to be civilized somewhere along the line by a professional trainer, or at least by a sensible mother who understood that strict obedience was *sine qua non* for children if they were to grow up to be good citizens.

In response to my grandmother's observations about the likelihood that she would fail miserably in all matters having to do with child-rearing, my mother promptly had not one, not two, but *three* children before the war, and two more in short order during the war, punctuated right after the war by Baby Heather in capital letters.

My grandmother was not amused, but at least Heather's birth had been followed by a "full stop" and not a comma.

Meanwhile, back in Berkeley, my grandmother surveyed with deep dissatisfaction the brood of children that had been placed under her unwilling care. One was autistic, one was highly intelligent but extremely introverted, and the third was a willful child with strong opinions that my grandmother didn't want to hear, especially coming from a two-year-old.

It didn't take her three minutes to make up her mind to hire a nanny.

The nanny turned out to be the infamous Miss Ava, the bane of our existence and a painful thorn in our sides. My grandmother interviewed a grand total of nine potential child torturers, and decided that Miss Ava was best suited for the job. The two women saw eye-to-eye on just about every tenet of strict Victorian child-rearing that came up in the interview. The two of them agreed on procedures that would have made Oliver Twist's life look quite enjoyable by comparison. Not only should children be seen and not heard, but they should never speak unless spoken to. We began living the life of Trappist monks, always involved in useful household labor and strongly discouraged from engaging in any form of idle talk.

This made life rather easy for my grandmother and her partner in crime, the redoubtable Miss Ava. Looking back on Miss Ava from my vantage point as an adult, I realize now that she must have been embittered by her spinsterhood and by the fact that she was obviously not suited for any of the really sought-after jobs, or why would she have ended up being a nanny when she had about as much love for children as Cruella De Vil had for the 101 Dalmatians? Miss Ava was unloved and unlovable, and as a result she was unloving as well. She probably had a very unhappy life herself, but the problem is that small children don't know anything about that. They just assume that the cold attitude and lack of affection on the part of the adults in their lives has something to do with *them.* They think they must have done something wrong, so they try harder to please. Usually this is a futile endeavor that ends up in total frustration.

This, at any rate, is the way I remembered our lives in Berkeley during the war. Would our visit to my old house be uplifting or depressing? It was hard for me to see how it could be the former. But Gordon seemed to be looking forward to seeing our old house, so off we went.

Rush hour was over, so it didn't take us long to get to 46 Domingo Avenue. At first the house looked unfamiliar to me, but as I continued to gaze at it, old memories began to come back to me. Believe it or not the "nesta" house was still there, comfortably ensconced in the front yard. What I had once called the nesta house was actually just a sizable clump of decorative tropical grass where I used to hide when I had my play time. It looked much smaller to me now than it did when I was a little girl, but it was still the nesta house—no doubt about it.

I remember one day when Craig was in school (and I was a preschooler), I decided to make a sweater for him by weaving together some strands of tall grass from the nesta house. I had a very clear vision, before I started the project, of how the grass sweater would turn out, but it didn't come close to matching the pattern in my head. Nevertheless, I decided to present my *chef d'oeuvre* to Craig when he got home from school, since I had worked on it for my entire play period, and I wanted him to see the final results.

I knew perfectly well it was just a jumbled piece of grassy nothingness, but I wanted to give it to him anyway. I expected him to take it, glance at it vaguely, and then toss it away later when he thought I wasn't looking. But to my astonishment he accept the gift with enormous gravitas and expressed deep appreciation for the lovely sweater, which he assured me he would wear to bed at night to keep him warm. I was bowled over. I wasn't fooled, but I was thrilled that he had played along with me and had pretended to be moved by my efforts on his behalf. Although Craig was no stranger to me, and although I had never heard of Blanche du Bois, her comment that she had always depended on the kindness of strangers would have resonated with me, although I would have preferred to substitute "brothers" for "strangers."

Another time I wanted to impress Craig with my great skill at writing the letters of the alphabet. I had been begging him for a long time to teach them to me, and I had been a diligent, meticulous student. We had now arrived at the letter "E." I assumed that the number of horizontal bars attached to the vertical one was supposed to be left entirely to the discretion of the individual writer. I thought it was Craig's opinion that three horizontal bars were all I could master at the age of three, and I was determined to show him that I could do much better than that.

So with great accuracy I carefully fashioned a letter "E" with eight horizontal bars instead of just three, and proudly showed it to Craig when he got home from school. At first he couldn't figure out what it was supposed to be (a comb, perhaps?), but after I explained to him what I had done, he pretended to be greatly impressed not only with the letter "E" I had made, but with my astonishing mathematical skill as well. I looked up at him and beamed, not wanting him to guess that I had no idea what a mathematical skill was.

"You see," Craig said, thoughtfully contemplating the "E" for a much longer period of time than would normally be expected, "*I* drew an "E" for you that has three bars because you're three, and *you* drew an "E" for me that has eight bars, because I'm eight. I find that very interesting, don't you?"

"Yes," I said, nodding wisely.

Craig was kind enough not to leave it there. He strongly advised me to continue making "E's" with just three bars for the sake of the rest of humanity, since there was a law that said it had to be done that way. There was no punishment for breaking that law, but there would be consequences. If I changed the shape of the letters of the alphabet to suit my own taste, nobody would ever be able to decipher what I was writing, and if that happened, I'd never have the satisfaction of being understood. And if nobody understood me, nobody would want to bother to get to know me better, so life would be lonely and probably rather unfulfilling as well. It seems to me, as I look back on the situation, that anyone sincerely contemplating a career in the arts or communication should take my brother's advice very seriously.

I smile when I think of Craig and the strange things we used to talk about with such intensity. My shy, introverted, intelligent brother had inherited Primrose's kind heart. But I wasn't aware of that at the time, since Primrose had not yet appeared on the horizon.

Gordon had been driving along Domingo Avenue and had come to a stop in front of number 49.

"Why don't you knock on the front door, Sonia, and see if anybody's home?" he suggested.

"Okay, let's give it a try."

The door was opened by a white-haired lady wearing a carefully ironed pink blouse with white slacks and tennis shoes. When I explained to her who I was and why we were there, she opened the door wider and asked us to come in.

I braced myself for an overwhelming experience, but it didn't turn out that way. It was exciting to see the first house I could ever remember living in, and it was comforting to see that the rooms were still the same. Nobody had knocked out walls or made other major adjustments. The furniture was different, of course, and that gave the interior an unfamiliar feel. The rooms seemed much smaller, too, but otherwise everything was still essentially the same as before.

"Please, just make yourselves at home," said the lady in the tennis shoes. "That sounds funny, doesn't it? You *are* at home. Well, at least you were here before I was, anyway."

"We won't stay long," I told her. "I don't want to get in the way. I'm sure you have things to do. But I did want to see what it felt like to be here again."

"And how *does* it feel?" she asked me. "I've never gone back to my childhood home, so I don't know what it's like."

"It's like meeting someone you haven't seen in years. You feel awkward because you don't know where to begin. You feel shy because you don't know who they are anymore. You feel excited because there's something poignant about the stages of life, especially as you near the end. So I guess I have to say that I feel this poignancy the same way as I would if I'd met someone I'd known long ago. But I realize that it would take time to explore and deepen the feelings that this house gives me, just as it would if I wanted to renew an old friendship with someone from the past."

"Well, that makes sense," she smiled. "I appreciate your taking the trouble to explain."

My sister Sheila was the person whose presence seemed most palpable in the house of our childhood. Maybe that was because she spent a lot of time explaining to me where things belonged, and why they had to be positioned just the right way. She knew every nook and cranny in the house, and had gone to great lengths to make me aware of the many details she had seen and memorized.

But as far as I was concerned, Sheila stood out in my memory for entirely different reasons. Although I was more of a perfectionist than the average person and could therefore appreciate her concern for detail, there was one thing about her that really touched my heart—nobody, but *nobody* could make her tell on Craig or me, no matter how hard they tried. She wouldn't lie, either, but if Miss Ava tried to pry some information out of her about something we had done that was against the rules, Sheila would clamp her mouth shut and just refuse to talk. She would take any punishment that Miss Ava could mete out, accepting it in stoic silence. She would skip dinner, she would go to her room, she would do extra household chores, but she wouldn't squeal on us.

Craig and I would threaten to confess our dreadful deeds so she'd be let off the hook, but Sheila wouldn't hear of it. We knew better than to interfere with her, for the frustration she would have felt if we'd imposed ourselves on her would have been more unbearable for her than our guilt would have been for us. Some people might have thought she was being a martyr, but it wasn't like that. She never played games.

What Sheila taught me went beyond a lesson in honor and fair play, although that was important, too. But what intrigued me most was the idea that punishment can be borne without fear, for the suffering that accompanies it is never quite as bad as we expect, especially when we're suffering for the sake of somebody else. What I learned from Sheila was the meaning of bravery and generosity of spirit. And she had a place for them, a very neatly arranged place for each of these virtues in her big, uncalculating heart.

Then right in the middle of this bleak and silent life under the watchful eye of my disgruntled grandmother and the embittered Miss Ava, along came Percy Pond to light up our lives and turn the night into day. He loved us, and we loved him back. He showered us with affection, and we responded with blissful joy. We competed for his attention, blooming like desert wildflowers after a sudden rainfall.

"Don't be spoiling those children," my grandmother said sternly. "I have enough to worry about as it is."

My grandfather tried to show her that he respected her wishes, but he would always give us a little wink and a smile when she wasn't looking. We were delighted. We had never been in cahoots with a grownup before, and it filled us with new hope for a better future.

Percy Pond was not the kind of man who liked to spend his time indoors. The day after he arrived he decided to take us kids on a nice long walk up into the Berkeley hills, so he gingerly approached my grandmother with the proposal.

"That's the most ridiculous idea I've ever heard," she stated categorically. "You're much too old to exert yourself that way, and Sonia's too young for such a walk. Sheila will wander off and get lost, and you can't expect *Craig* to be in charge. He's only ten."

But Percy had insisted, and my grandmother had finally relented, after laying down a list of stipulations. He had cheerfully accepted all her rules and regulations, and off we went to the hills, leaving my grandmother feeling secretly pleased at the prospect of having a little quiet time to herself.

That was the day the prisoners were released. It was a day of perfect, splendid freedom—our day in the sun. We ran, we jumped, we lay down on our backs, we laughed, we talked, we asked questions, we picked flowers, we ate tuna sandwiches on a boulder. And then it was time to go home.

We burst into the house and ran to Granny, vying with one another to be the first to tell her about our glorious day in the hills. We knew she wouldn't like to be assaulted that way, but we were hoping that our enthusiasm would be contagious, and that she would understand at last how happy we children could be if she would only let us go on a picnic once in a while, or even just a nice walk in the hills *without* the tuna sandwiches if they were too much trouble.

But our efforts fell on deaf ears. My grandmother was grimly determined to put an immediate stop to what she feared would be a growing interest on our part to "run wild," so she sent us off to bed to "settle down." We spent our naptime reliving the splendor of our hike with Percy Pond, the talented photographer who celebrated the beauty of God's natural world by making it a gift to his grandchildren.

"What year was that, do you know?" Gordon asked me.

"It was 1943. I was five years old."

He looked at me thoughtfully for a moment.

"Didn't we read somewhere that your grandfather died that year?"

I suddenly felt flushed with an indescribable emotion as it dawned on me that Primrose had come to Berkeley to say farewell. All at once I was gripped by that familiar sense of heart-wrenching poignancy. Percy Pond had wanted to see his wife and meet his grandchildren before he took his final curtain. He was not a man of means, so I knew he must have spent his last dollar on the expensive journey from Juneau to San Francisco. The man my grandmother called a dreamer, the man she had called "absurdly impractical," the man she had criticized for his ineffectual attempts to put sufficient quantities of bread on the table—that same man had dreamed the absurdly impractical dream of spending everything he had to bid farewell to the people he loved the most. I hoped my gentle, poetic grandfather understood that the truth would eventually become clear to those loved ones. I hoped that he was smiling down on me then, happy in the knowledge that I'd rediscovered him in our old haunts.

I did my best to express these thoughts to Gordon, who was striving hard to understand Percy Pond, this well-known photographer, this son of Juneau who had become so famous without even trying, and without ever knowing he had even reached such unexpected heights.

The white-haired lady in the tennis shoes invited us to have tea with her before we left that afternoon. She listened spellbound to the story of Percy Pond, then summarized it in a few words as we were thanking her and taking our leave at the front door of 46 Domingo Avenue.

"There's a nice symmetry in your story," she observed. "Percy Pond traveled *away* from Juneau to a faraway city to say farewell to his family, and you traveled *to* Juneau and Berkeley from a distant Canadian province to say hello to him. They weren't really what you'd call practical journeys, either of them. They were more like journeys of the heart."

That's what life had been for Primrose—a journey of the heart. That phrase reflected the very essence of his sensitive, artistic nature, captured in just a few quick brush strokes by a perfect stranger.

CHAPTER NINE

Life returned to normal for us at 46 Domingo Avenue when Primrose went back home to Alaska. I tried my best to obediently resume the Trappist life of silence, but I had lost the habit of keeping quiet while Primrose was around. He had uncorked in me a previously undiscovered reservoir of non-stop chatter, so after he left I began to break the rule of silence with distressing regularity.

One day when I was walking along the sidewalk on the way to the grocery store with my grandmother, I noticed two men digging a big hole in the street with some very loud jack hammers. It was an unusually hot day, and the men were perspiring profusely. When I paused to see what they were doing, they decided to take a little break and chat for a while with this sweet little old lady and her toddler.

"You look nice and cool in your sun suit," one of the men said to me, wiping his brow with his arm.

I was proudly wearing a tiny little pink one-piece cotton outfit with straps over my bare shoulders and lace around the edges, topped off with a pink bonnet to match. He, on the other hand, was in a long-sleeved blue shirt and heavy denim overalls. He was obviously much more covered up than I was, and I could easily see why he would be feeling hot and unhappy. The solution seemed simple to me.

"Why don't *you* wear a sun suit too, then?" I asked him.

The men thought about this for a moment, then broke out in loud howls of unrestrained laughter.

My grandmother looked at them with an apologetic grin, as if to say, "you'll have to excuse her, she's only a child." Then she took my hand and hurried me down the sidewalk, saying "how many times have I told you not to ask silly questions?" while the men's laughter rang in my ears.

For the first time in my life I didn't feel worried by the fact that I was in trouble with my grandmother again. I had discovered that day that it's enormously gratifying to make people laugh. What a marvelous counterpoint to an otherwise grim and humorless existence!

When my grandmother finally got tired of telling me to hush up, she decided (for once in her life) to take the path of least resistance by marching off to the library and checking out a copy of Rudyard Kipling's *Just So Stories*, which were perfect for answering my constant questions about how the world functioned. Stories such as *How the Whale Got His Throat, How the Camel Got His Hump, How the Rhinoceros Got His Skin,* and *Why the Sea Is Salt* were so exciting to me that my grandmother was able to get me to bed in record time every night. If I was "all settled" by exactly seven o'clock, she would come to my bedroom and read me one of those stories. If Sheila and Craig had been good all day, they were invited to join us as well.

This little ritual satisfied my grandmother in two ways. She was a teacher, first of all, so she didn't find the task displeasing. And secondly, it proved to her that the carrot was more effective than the stick. It's hard to imagine why it took her so long to make this world-shaking discovery, but I suppose it had something to do with her basic personality. Strict disciplinarians of the Victorian variety were attracted by the necessity of meting out punishment, but when Granny got old she found it tiresome to have to put up with screams and tears of protestation, so she decided to loosen her grip and allow the carrot to do its work. We all benefited greatly from this more relaxed approach to the challenge of bringing us up properly, and we went to bed in a better frame of mind for sleeping.

The Just So Stories were one small step for the first three Harrison children, but the giant step was taken by my father, who was by his very nature incapable of taking steps of any other size. When Germany surrendered on May 8th, 1945, the first thing my father did was book a passage to America so that he could gather up his children and take them home to England.

The news spread like wildfire through the house at 46 Domingo Avenue. Craig was the first to tell me.

"The war's over, Sonia! Daddy's coming!"

"He's coming here?"

"Yes, and he's going to take us home!"

"Home where?"

"Home to England. Where Mummy lives."

"Who's Mummy again?"

"She's our mother. And she's very nice. She's not a bit like Granny or Miss Ava. You're going to *love* her."

I stopped and thought for a while. The only women I had known in the family setting were Granny and Miss Ava, and they didn't seem very nice to me. But I had liked the women who had been my teachers at the John Muir School, so I naturally concluded that women who were caretakers were not nice, but women who were teachers were terrific.

"Is Mummy a teacher?"

"No, she's just Mummy."

"Well, what's she like?"

"She's very pretty, and she dresses in beautiful clothes. She's gentle and kind and she smiles a lot. She'll never punish you, and she'll never tell you to hush up."

"Well, who's going to tell me to hush up, then?"

"Don't worry, Granny will still be around. She's going to live with us again."

"Is Miss Ava coming too?"

"No. She's staying here."

"Hooray!" I shouted, feeling for the first time in my life the glorious relief of being able to cast away a heavy burden.

"Oh, hush up!" came my grandmother's voice from a distant corner of the house. "What's all the fuss about?"

"The war's over!" I cried, running to find her. "Daddy's coming here to take us to *England!*"

"Why did you have to tell her all about that, Craig?" my grandmother said as we approached her. "Now I'm going to have to put up with all her questions until he gets here. And it could be *weeks!*"

I feel a bit guilty talking about my grandmother as if she were stern and grumpy from the minute she got out of bed in the morning till she turned out the lights at night. She really wasn't that bad. Not all the time, anyway. I can remember very clearly at least two instances when she was both brave and kind, and jumped immediately to my defense.

The first time was at the end of the second grade, when I was walking through the schoolyard at the back of the John Muir School on my way home. Suddenly Dick Egan popped up from nowhere and grabbed my arm. He and a couple of other boys pulled me roughly over to the jungle gym and held me prisoner there. No matter how hard I tried, I couldn't pull away from him. I felt scared, but I was curious to know what on earth he was doing, and what he had in mind. Why would anyone want to latch onto a jungle gym with one hand and then hold onto a classmate with the other so she couldn't go anywhere? I stared at him until he finally spoke.

"You think you're so smart," he sneered.

"No I don't. What are you talking about?"

"You think you're so smart," he said again. Then he looked at his buddies and laughed. They laughed too, just to go along with him, but I had the feeling they didn't know what was so funny.

"Let me *go!*"

"You're stayin' right here," he said.

"I have to go home!"

"You're not goin' nowheres."

"My grandmother will get mad at me."

"Good."

"You're going to get in trouble."

My heart began to beat faster. There was a long silence while Dick tried to come up with something devastating to say to me. I could see the cogs and wheels turning.

"You think you're so smart," he said yet again.

Why did he keep saying that? It's true I loved school. It was the greatest place in the world. You could ask as many questions as you liked, and the teachers were always nice. I would sit in the front row and put my hand up to answer her questions. It was like being on *The Quiz Kids* every day. It was the exact opposite of home, and I was in heaven.

"You think you're so smart," came Dick Egan's voice again. He breathed the words into my ear in a low, guttural voice and threatening tone.

"What's *wrong* with you?" I asked him.

"What's wrong with *you?*" was the brilliant come-back.

I began to cry. Yes, you women out there, you can all be very disappointed in me. I wimped out. But I was only seven years old, remember, and I was facing three big bullies who were much stronger than I was. Besides, you don't know my grandmother. If I was late getting home, I was always in big trouble.

"I'm going to tell my dad."

"You don't have a dad. Everybody knows that."

"Yes I *do!* He's coming to get me."

"Yeah? When?"

"Soon."

"Soon, she says."

He and his goons laughed again.

Much to his great satisfaction I cried harder, out of pure frustration and rage. Eventually he got tired of his little game and he let me go. I galloped home and told my grandmother between heaving sobs what Dick Egan had done.

"You stay right here," she said, marching out of the house and slamming the door behind her.

The next thing I knew she was back again, dragging Dick Egan along by the collar.

"Apologize," she barked at him.

"Sorry," he said softly.

"I didn't hear you!"

"Sorry," he said, with a hangdog look.

"What are you sorry about?" my grandmother asked.

"I'm sorry I kept her after school."

"Why did you do it?"

"She thinks she's so smart."

"Oh, so what that really means is that *you* think you're stupid. Well, if you studied your lessons you wouldn't feel so stupid. How about trying *that* for a change?"

"All right."

"All right *what?*"

"All right, I'll study my lessons."

"All right, *Ma'am,*" my grandmother bellowed. "When you talk to me you'll address me as *Ma'am.*"

"Yes, Ma'am."

"And if I ever catch you near my granddaughter again, there's going to be *hell* to pay. Is that clear?"

"Yes, Ma'am."

"Now get out of here. Run along home."

My grandmother said *hell!* What if he reported her to a policeman? Or a minister? What would a minister say to *that?* And what if Dick Egan hated me now, and decided to do something even worse to get back at me?

I needn't have worried. I never saw Dick Egan again.

Years later, when the internet came out, I looked for him on all the search engines. But Richard Egan was nowhere to be found. He had simply disappeared from the face of the earth.

The second time my grandmother was brave and came straight to my rescue was a much scarier situation than the one involving Dick Egan. I woke up late one night to find a strange man standing at the side of my bed looking down at me. At first I thought he was a friend of my grandmother's who had decided to come in and check on me. I greeted him and told him I was all right, but he didn't respond. He just kept looking at me without saying anything. I began to feel scared. People don't just stand there without answering you when you speak. I asked who he was, and he didn't answer. I asked him why he was there, and he still wouldn't answer. Finally I sat up in bed and just stared at him. He stared right back, unashamed and unembarrassed. He stared at me with a sort of scientific interest, as if I were a rare insect pinned in a display case.

I began to cry, but he didn't care. I cried louder, and he didn't flinch. I began to cry hysterically, but this only gave him more to think about as he continued with his scientific investigation of my insectitude. I was scared of him not so much because he was a stranger in my bedroom, but because he didn't give a hoot about how upset I was. I could tell that he had no heart, and I found that terrifying.

Eventually I could hear my grandmother coming up the stairs. I know he heard her footsteps too, but he didn't even look around. He knew perfectly well he was in full control of the situation, and he wasn't in the least bit concerned that my formidable grandmother, the purveyor of all punishment, was on the way.

He seemed to crouch slightly as she came up the stairs, the way a fly might crouch just before you take a swipe at it with your hand. It sees you coming and it somehow sets its legs, then springs up and flies away just before you can catch it. Well, that man's legs were set just the same way. So the moment my grandmother opened my bedroom door, he sprang into the air and flew horizontally out the window, leaving me to explain to my exasperated grandmother why I was crying hysterically over nothing.

I told her between uncontrollable sobs exactly what had happened, but I didn't tell her that the man had flown out the window. She was brave enough to look for him in all the possible places where he could be hiding. Then she checked the other rooms on the second floor, but she found nothing.

Finally she came back to my room and told me that I had had a bad dream.

"It wasn't a dream!" I objected. "He was really there! He was standing right next to my bed, staring at me! And he had no heart and no feelings. Nothing! He was *horrible!*"

She looked at me quizzically for a moment.

"It was just a bad dream," she insisted. "You must have been dreaming about Dick Egan."

"He wasn't Dick Egan. He was a bad man, and he was real! He was standing right there where you are now."

She gave me a drink of water and sat by my bed until I finally fell asleep.

I admired my grandmother for being so brave, and I'm grateful to her now for taking care of us kids at a time in her life when she would much rather have been retired and trouble-free. But I never, ever forgot the man who didn't know how to love, and for the rest of my life I understood that the absence of love is the very definition of pure evil.

Some people might think I created this bad man in my imagination because of a sort of deep-seated fear of men, brought about by the lack of a father figure in my early life. But this is the very opposite of the truth. I had met Primrose by then, and he was one of the most unforgettable characters I had ever known. If I could have wrapped him up and sent him to the *Reader's Digest,* I would have done so. Nobody with Primrose for a grandfather could possibly have had anything against men. Then my father came along after the war, and my opinion of men went right over the moon.

He arrived at our house one day in early June, 1945. Sheila and Craig recognized him immediately, and they ran up to him and hugged him. Well, Craig did, but Sheila hung back for a while until she was ready to hug him, but she eventually did. My grandmother recognized him too, and she also hugged him. She must have liked him very much, because I don't remember her hugging anyone ever before. Not even Primrose.

When my turn came my father got right down on his haunches and looked me straight in the eyes.

"I'm never going to let you out of my sight, ever again!" he declared.

"Never?" I asked him dubiously, thinking about all the complications involved in never letting someone out of your sight for the rest of your life.

"Come on, we're going for a walk. I want you to show me the neighborhood."

"Don't be too long, Kay," my grandmother warned him. "Dinner is at six."

"We're all going out for dinner tonight. I'm taking you to the Claremont Hotel."

"We can't do that," she said. "The children have to be in bed by seven."

"We can do anything we like. We're going to break all the rules. We're going to run amok through the town."

"You'll spoil them, Kay. You'll undo all my work."

"They're *my* children," he reminded her, "and I'm going to spoil them rotten."

I sucked in my breath. Nobody had ever spoken to my grandmother that way. What would she say?

"My, my! You're such a rogue, Kay," she purred.

We had dinner at the Claremont Hotel with white table cloths, heavy silverware, waiters in starched shirts, a fish with googly eyes staring at us from a platter, and dishes piled high with ice cream and cake for dessert. I was so full I could barely walk, but I'd never felt happier except on the day when Percy Pond took us to the Berkeley hills.

"Why are these children so quiet?" I heard my dad say to my grandmother after we were supposed to be asleep that evening. "What's wrong with them, anyway? They hardly ever talk. They don't behave like children at all."

"You should be proud of your children," she declared. "They're polite, well behaved, and respectful. They'll make a good impression wherever they go."

"Yes, but where's their creativity? And where's their imagination? They need to be exposed to everything that life has to offer. They need to be passionate about what they do and see and learn. They're Harrisons, after all!"

The next morning my father explained that he was going to assign us our own personal special day to do exactly as we pleased. The other two could share our day with us, and that way we would all get to have three days of bliss and glory before it was time to board the train for the East Coast.

I thought I had died and gone to heaven. My father put me up on his shoulders and showed me the world from a brand new perspective. We went to the beach and made sand castles with moats and towers. We went wading in the cold, soft sand, and we watched the otters eating shellfish while they floated on their backs. We had lunch at the Cliff House, and listened to the seals barking at one another on the rocks. We went to the zoo and fed the tapirs and heard a lion roar. It was so loud I could feel the sound vibrate in my tummy. We went to an amusement park and crashed into one another with bumper cars, and waved happily at the rest of the world from the top of a Ferris wheel. All these things were a brand new experience for me.

Just as Primrose had shown us the quiet, natural beauty of the Berkeley hills, my father introduced us to the joys of man-made excitement. The country mouse and the city mouse had combined their efforts to provide us a panoramic view of the world that we had never known while we were locked up in our house at 46 Domingo Avenue. Our horizons were expanding, along with our ability to appreciate the full landscape. My grandmother had taught us discipline and hard work, Primrose had taught us to appreciate natural beauty, and my father, in just three glorious days, filled us with the desire to throw ourselves passionately into the arms of life without fear or reservation. It remained for us to put it all together and watch it bloom.

The following photographs are from the Historical Collection of the Alaska State Library.

Percy Pond (1872-1943) stands on the dock in Juneau, Alaska. ASL-PCA 87-1273

Lloyd Winter (left) and Percy Pond stand in the doorway of their Front Street studio in Juneau, Alaska, ca. 1900.

The Winter and Pond company store in the Horseshoe Building on South Main Street
ASL-P87-0985

Bart Thane, mining engineer and entrepreneur
ASL-P87-2398

Lloyd Winter, partner of Edwin Percy Pond
ASL-P297-330

The interior of the Winter and Pond studio, with a fur rug and a garden trellis backdrop. A camera is in the right fore ground, and a stool with a back rest and neck support is in front of the screen. ASL-P87-0991

A landslide on January 2, 1920 destroys the Winter and Pond photo studio. ASL-P87-1219

Percy Pond sits in his apartment on South Franklin Street, where the partners established their new photo studio. Pictures of Percy's son, Edwin, and his daughter, Marion Belle, are on the wall. These photos were taken in San Francisco in the mid 1920's, when Edwin was a graphic artist and Marion Belle was at the University of California at Berkeley. PCA-87-1275

Interior of the Winter and Pond Building on South Franklin Street ASL-P87-0996

Percy Pond (left) and Lloyd Winter at Taku Glacier
ASL-P87-1280

Percy Pond (left) and Harriet Hall Pond with John Davies, at their log cabin, "Hotel Scotia," 1899
ASL-P87-1270

Percy Pond (center, above steps) and Hattie Hall Pond (center, long white dress) stand on front porch, surrounded by friends. John Davies is probably holding baby Edwin, as the year is 1900.

ASL-P87-0731

Eight-year-old Edwin Pond (top row, 4th from left) with third-grade classmates in Juneau's public school, June 3rd, 1907

ASL-P226-187

*Log cabin church at Third and Main Streets; the Reverend J.H.
Condit (whom Edwin called "the Spiddit") and probably his wife
and daughter stand by the door.* ASL-P87-1105

Indian village in Howkan, Alaska, ca. 1897 ASL-Howkan-10

Bart Thane was responsible for the creation of the Salmon Creek Dam and reservoir. Thane's designer was Lars Jorgensen, and his chief engineer was Harry L. Wallenberg. This was the first true constant-angle arch dam; it is 168 feet high and 648 feet across. It was completed in 1914.　　　ASL-P87-1429

Percy Pond writes: "The success of this mine [Thane's Alaska-Juneau Gold Mining Co.] is the greatest triumph in the history of gold mining. In this mill over 8,000 tons of ore are handled daily at an average cost of 41½ cents per ton." ASL-P87-0517

Jacob's Ladder, a portage in the canyon near Sheep Camp, Alaska, ca. 1898. Three men pull sleds up a narrow log bridge. Man facing camera might be John Davies. ASL-P87-0675

Chautauqua party at Mendenhall Glacier, Juneau, Alaska, Sept. 23rd, 1921 ASL-P87-2597

Chilkat chiefs in dancing costumes, Klukwan, Alaska
ASL-P117-172

Two Tlingit Indian girls, Juneau, Alaska. Carved totem fish and part of totemic drawing on wall, ca. 1900   ASL-P87-0070

Chilkat Indian and blanket, Alaska   ASL-P87-0039

A woman and her son stand in front of a Chilkat dancing blanket. They are posing in the studio of Alaska frontier photographers Lloyd Winter and Percy Pond.

ASL-P87-0297

One-legged fisherman totem by fenced graves and marker, "In memory of Kaukish, died 1897 Age 68 Yrs." ca 1905

ASL-P87-0134

Alaska State Library - Historical Collections

Haida Indians in ceremonial dress outside Dogfish house in Klinkwan, ca 1900   ASL-P87-0318

Evergreen Cemetery, Juneau Alaska. Burial place of the founding pioneers of the State of Alaska.
Photo credit: www.answers.com/topic/evergreen-cemetery

CHAPTER TEN

It was time for Gordon and me to pack our things, check out of the St. Francis Hotel, and go back home to Nova Scotia. The journey of the heart that had taken us to Alaska and to the San Francisco Bay Area was now a new part of my life. The jigsaw puzzle was starting to take shape, and my anticipation was increasing as I gradually worked my way toward the middle, adding pieces here and there as I went along. The speed was picking up as things began to make more and more sense, and my excitement was growing apace.

As we winged our way over majestic purple mountains and amber waves of grain, I was reminded of another trip in 1945 that had also propelled my father and the "Berkeley" Harrisons from sea to shining sea. When he'd come to get us after the war he'd booked us onto one of the new streamliner passenger trains that had America all agog. The interstate highway system had not yet been completed and there was little competition from air traffic at the time, so a good deal of money had been pumped into the manufacture of the most luxurious trains the world had ever known.

We kids had the time of our lives. Granny, Sheila, and I shared a private compartment, and Dad and Craig were in the one next door. The two compartments were mirror images of each other, and both of them were big enough to seat all five of us if we wanted to be together. There was a table that could be rigged up between the seats so we could play games or write letters or even have a meal, but Granny said it was better for us to eat in the dining car which, after all, had been specially designed for that purpose.

We were allowed to explore the whole train as much as we wanted, whenever we wanted, for as long as we wanted, provided we didn't "make a nuisance of ourselves." When I asked my father what that meant exactly, he replied that it would be much better for us not to run up and down the aisles with a steaming hot bowl of spaghetti with marinara sauce, just in case the train lurched and sent us reeling right onto the ample bosom of a well-dressed society lady who had just settled down for a little nap. We loved it when Dad spelled things out for us that way.

The train was full of servicemen who had fought in the Pacific and were now coming home from the war. I quickly learned that they were friendly young men, and they didn't seem to mind talking to a seven-year-old chatterbox who had just been released from a five-year vow of silence and could not stop talking no matter how hard she tried.

It turned out to be a rather nice thing for Craig, who was too shy to approach any strangers. So I'd be the one to make friends with the soldiers, and then I would introduce them to my brother. The conversation would then climb immediately to a higher level, much to everyone's great satisfaction. I didn't mind—I was already talking to the next soldier in my line-up of victims. I hoped this wasn't what Granny meant when she warned me not to make a nuisance of myself.

Sheila wasn't interested in exploring the train or talking to the soldiers. She spent her time sitting in the compartment studying her astronomy books. She liked being in this little room because it was compact and intelligently arranged, with nothing out of place as far as she could tell. She liked the stars for the same reason. She found it deeply gratifying that they were always exactly where they were supposed to be, precisely when they were meant to be there.

When we arrived on the East Coast we spent a couple of days in a house with a towering man called Senator Hawkes, in Montclair, New Jersey. The house was huge, and it had marble floors everywhere, both inside and out. I don't recall much about our visit except that Mr. Hawkes was friendly and down-to-earth, in spite of his height. The one thing I do remember is being scared to death of the two bulldogs that patrolled the hallways. I had never seen a bulldog before, and I thought their loose skin and pushed-in faces made them the ugliest creatures on earth.

Apparently they loved little children. At least, that's what Mr. Hawkes told me later. They had spotted me from somewhere in the distance and had come galloping over as fast as they could, wanting to greet me with great, slobbering licks and kisses. They slid and slipped all over the marble floors, and when they finally reached me they banged right into my legs and knocked me down. They hadn't meant any harm—they just couldn't stop, that's all. But I was hurt and scared, and I set up a wail that brought Mr. Hawkes running. I cringed when I saw this gigantic man rushing toward me, for I was afraid that he'd slip on the marble floor too and run me down like a streamliner passenger train, but luckily he was able to stop in time. He scooped me up and held me way up over the dogs' heads while they jumped up on him as high as they could go, barking excitedly and lunging for my feet. I remember feeling sorry for Mr. and Mrs. Hawkes, having to live in the same house with such affectionate dogs.

After we thanked the Hawkes for having us, we went to the dock to board the ship that would take us to England. I don't remember how long it took to get there—I only know that I spent the whole time thinking about those bulldogs and wondering if they knew what the word "hawk" meant. If they did, I thought maybe it might explain why they were so excitable. I asked Sheila what she thought about my idea, but she doubted that they had such an extensive vocabulary.

I also remember being fascinated by the sound of certain words when they were put together and spoken out loud. I didn't know how to express the idea of rhythm or alliteration or rhyming syllables, so I simply asked Sheila what the words meant.

"What are *dimples* and *steeples,* Sheila?"

"Well, dimples are those little indentations that people have on their cheeks or chins, and steeples are the pointed towers on top of churches."

"I know, but what are dimples and steeples when you put them *together?"*

"Steeples don't have dimples, and dimples don't have steeples, so they can't be together," Sheila said.

"But why do they sound so interesting when you *say* them together?"

"Oh hush up, Sonia," said my grandmother impatiently. "Leave your sister alone."

"Sheila," I said in her ear so Granny couldn't hear me. "Did you know that I was *sick* when I was *six?"*

"You were sick every year, not just when you were six," she whispered back.

The staterooms on the *Aquitania* were even bigger than the compartments on the train, and there was plenty of room on board for us to run around all day and never finish seeing everything there was to see. The dining room was huge, the food was delicious, and hide-and-seek on the *Aquitania* was the best thing any child could wish for. I don't remember any soldiers being on board—maybe because we were going in the wrong direction as far as they were concerned. Most of them were American or Canadian soldiers coming home from the European front, but we were going the other way. Soon we would be in England, and that was the country *we* would be calling "home."

On the last day of the voyage my father brought out some clothes that my mother had packed for us to wear when we reached Southampton. He explained to us that they were called "kilts," and the plaid design was called a "tartan" that represented the Morrison family in Scotland from which his mother descended. So we got all decked out in these kilts with a sporran in front, and tweed jackets and patent leather shoes with big silver buckles. It was customary, Dad said, for people to dress formally for debarking.

"But I can't wear a skirt," said Craig, looking mortified.

"Scottish men have been doing it for centuries," my dad assured him, "and they're all very burly, masculine fellows with nice thick calf muscles. They wear kilts to go hunting, and even to go to war. So don't worry, you won't look like a sissy. And you can wear your Y-fronts underneath."

"What are Y-fronts?"

"You know, your underpants, or briefs, or whatever you want to call them."

"I call them briefs."

"Good. So if anyone asks you what a Scotsman wears under his kilt, you can tell them he wears briefs."

"Why would anyone ask me *that?*"

"Because people are silly, that's all."

When we got to Southampton we three kids became the center of attention for journalists and photographers looking for stories about refugee children on their way home after the war. Our Scottish getups provided a nice angle for the news hounds and the paparazzi. One thing I learned about my dad that day—he always knew how to attract publicity without appearing to be looking for it. What Craig learned was that public attention can be annoying and sometimes downright embarrassing. He must have been asked at least a dozen times what he was wearing under his kilt.

A car from my father's office was waiting for us when we got out of customs. We were introduced to Thornley, the chauffeur, who loaded our suitcases into the boot and then drove us home to 49 Charles Street. This brings me back to the part of the jigsaw puzzle I'd been working on before, when I was remembering how Josy had stepped forward to greet us when we got there, while my mother hung back and watched the scene from the front door of the house.

Why had Josy, our housekeeper and stand-in nanny, been so effusive in her welcome while my mother had just looked on from the background? Why hadn't my mother hugged us or kissed us? Was she so shy that she couldn't find the courage to come and say hello to her own children, who had been gone for five years? Was she so afraid of her feelings that she didn't dare to come forward? Did she think we'd resent her for sending us away and not coming with us to California during the war? Did she think we'd wonder why she had two *more* children during the war if it was so unsafe for us to live in London ourselves?

All I knew was that whenever I thought *I* was in trouble, I would also avoid joining any family activities until I felt it was safe to come out. Nobody likes to make the first move if they think they'll be spurned. It's like hesitating to say you're sorry to someone if you think they're going to turn around and say, "Well, you *should* be!"

Still, I'm surprised that my mother didn't seem to know that little kids don't judge grownups as a rule. Not when they're very young. They take it for granted that the adults in their world know exactly what they're doing and always make the right decisions. You have to reach adolescence before you discover the joy of blaming your parents for all your problems, and I hadn't quite arrived at that exalted state just then. It hadn't yet occurred to me to blame her for anything at all. But the day she had probably dreaded right from the beginning finally arrived ten years later, when I *did* blame her for sending us away.

My questions got darker and more hostile as I got older, so my mother decided to send me to a psychologist. The psychologist, however, only made matters worse by telling me that my mother's decision to send us away had caused us great harm by making the three of us feel unloved. This had created abandonment issues that I would have to deal with sooner or later if I wanted to be healthy enough to have a successful marriage of my own some day. It was her job, she explained, to help me see all the many complexities that I hadn't noticed before, and which would come back to haunt me later on if I didn't face them and come to grips with them as quickly as possible.

It would have been a good thing for both my mom and me if she had taken the time to assure me that my mother had done her best to make the right decision for us, and that any decision she might have made could have had undesirable consequences, because life is full of pain and sorrow and we all have to learn to deal with it without blaming anyone else, which is essentially a waste of time. But she didn't say that, so I ended up thinking that my mother had very cavalierly made a terrible decision for me which had left me wounded and damaged, and now *I* was going to have to struggle with it and pay the price for it while she went on her merry way.

I began to act as though my mother had found me caught in an animal trap in the woods, but had decided to cut off my foot rather than figure out how to open the trap, because she didn't love me enough to make the effort. It was *my* foot, after all, and not hers, so why should *she* care? The worst of it was that I suspected she thought I was exaggerating when I told her that it was hard to get along in life without a foot. I had the feeling that she believed she had only scratched my foot, and she was clinging to that belief because she felt less guilty that way. It was convenient for her to be "in denial," as the psychologist called it when she had refused to admit her so-called guilt in this whole matter. *I* had to pay with my foot so *she* could feel guilt-free, I thought. I was well on my way to becoming a blamer rather than a problem-solver.

I faced her one day with my litany of complaints. I was rather proud of myself for having the courage to do so, and I fully believed that if she apologized to me I would then be able to forgive her and get started with the healing process. But it turned out that she felt very hurt by my own cavalier attitude to the difficult position she had been in. She had had to choose between her children and her husband, and it had been a veritable *Sophie's Choice*. Now here I was, standing there telling her she had ruined my life!

"What about Granny?" I asked her, a glint of triumphant insight shining in my eyes. "You never got along with her, so is this why you wouldn't come with us to Berkeley? Is that why you decided to stay behind, so you could let *us* deal with your mother for a change, while you had a holiday?"

But my mother wasn't having any of *that*. Her mother had had to give up her well-deserved retirement to take care of three children when she was in her seventies. Didn't I feel any gratitude for that?

I brought up the subject of Miss Ava, but that didn't get me any sympathy, either. My mother reminded me of how difficult it had been to find anyone to take care of children when there were so many jobs to do while the men were dying on the battle front. So if silence was the only torture I had endured, I should count myself lucky.

I stood my ground. I told her that I had the feeling that she had probably stayed in England so she could keep an eye on her philandering husband, a proposition to which she had readily agreed. And why shouldn't she have done so? Did I prefer the idea of a divorce and a broken family, with some gold-digging mistress taking the place of my real mother? She had held the family together at great cost to her own dignity. If I didn't think it was humiliating to play second fiddle to a mistress, then I didn't know anything at all!

We ended up calling a truce. My mother knew that it couldn't have been easy for me not to have a mom and dad till I was seven, but she would appreciate it if I could try to see it a little more from *her* point of view as well. I had to agree that the whole situation was more complicated than I had realized, but neither of us apologized and neither of us sought a hug from the other. We both went off in our own directions to nurse our wounded pride and to stew about how misunderstood and unappreciated we were. My mother was probably thinking how supremely unsatisfactory children can be sometimes, and I was definitely thinking that mothers are never concerned enough about their wounded, bleeding kids. *Stürm und drang* all around, but mainly on my end.

I began to wonder if I was engaging in a bit of a power play here. Did I want to get the upper hand over my mother by making demands and accusations? What could possibly be gained by that? What was *wrong* with me? I was an ungrateful brat who took what was given to me as though it were my due, *that's* what was wrong with me. I knew I had done nothing to deserve the many benefits I had been given in my life so far, including the safe haven in Berkeley.

Yet the brattiness lingered. I clung to the belief that I needed love and not protection money, but I was too young to realize to what extent love *is* money. When we give our children comfort and opportunity by paying for their needs, or when we protect their marriages from dissolving into a morass of bitter arguments over financial shortfalls, our help may come in the form of money, but the impulse to help is inspired by love, just as the urge to make the money in the first place is inspired partly by a desire to create a safety net for the sake of the children. We run the risk of spoiling them, perhaps, or causing them to become pitiful, helpless cases of arrested development (could that possibly have been *moi?*), but by keeping the wolf from their door we could be sparing them from a lifetime of the kind of hostility and acrimony that is capable of tearing families apart.

My mother once told me that growing up poor in Alaska was a very degrading experience for her. She had promised herself she would do everything in her power never to be poor again as long as she lived. She would make sure she married a man who was a good provider, if nothing else. Here is how she put it in one of her letters to me:

There are hard and cold facts in this frightening workaday modern world that we're forced to consider. Marriage is for a long time, and it's essential that the husband have ways and means of supporting his wife. Why should this be, when girls are able to support themselves in style nowadays? Because of the periods of enforced helplessness that will overtake you. Children come along, and so far it's still the husband who can make it possible for you to devote the necessary time to these sweet creatures who will need your care. It isn't satisfactory to have to run to a job, and leave these little helpless people in the hands of ignorant nannies. It would be heartbreaking to a mother, in that she wouldn't know how they were being treated. Better not to work, and care for them herself. In that case, whether she can eat or not depends entirely on the husband.

My mother probably experienced the heartbreak of not really knowing how we were being treated in Berkeley. Add to that the anguish of having a child who bitterly blames you for having chosen the lesser of two evils, and you have a broken mother, a mother who says, "I give up. No matter what I do, my best is never good enough."

I began to think about doing something to help her feel the joy of motherhood that she must have eagerly anticipated when she got married. I could start, I thought, by developing a more companionable relationship with her. We could sit down together and talk about life and human nature over our morning coffee. I could learn to see things from *her* point of view. It would be good to add this other dimension to what was probably my one-sided, adolescent, self-absorbed view of the world. I would begin to look at things in a new light. Maybe we could even add a little humor to the mix, to help shoo away the pain.

It sounded fine, but I ended up putting those plans on the back burner. The time had come for me to go to college (paid for by love money), and this opened up new vistas and turned me in other directions. There would be plenty of time later to repair the damage.

It never occurred to me that mothers don't live forever, or that my procrastination was largely due to the fact that I was still reveling in the joy of self-pity.

CHAPTER ELEVEN

If I thought life was difficult under the aegis of Miss Ava and my grandmother in California, the complexities of our new life in England were even more challenging. A lot of it had to do with the fact that we were all very young children and we had a hard time understanding things from the point of view of other people. Besides, there were so many points of view running around loose in the household that any effort to take them all into account would have been nearly impossible anyway.

First of all there was my grandmother, who had earned an honorable discharge from her service. She believed she deserved the equivalent of a medal for endurance in the line of duty, and she was ready now for the payback. Who could blame her? She was getting along in years, so now it was *her* turn to recline on a chaise longue and eat peeled grapes.

Then there was Josy, a lively, bustling Austrian refugee who had escaped from the Nazis after the Anschluss and had made her way to England, where my mom had hired her as a housekeeper and nanny for Wilda and Nigel. She was a bit of a mystery, as she refused to divulge any information at all about the family she had left behind, preferring instead to adopt *our* family and forget about the real one. I was much too young to understand that her attitude was a potential red flag, and my mother was too kindly to see it that way.

My mother always said that she was a godsend in that she could do the work of three people—cooking, cleaning, and caring for children. She never went anywhere without pushing a vacuum cleaner ahead of her with one hand while holding a pile of freshly folded laundry in the other. She was everywhere at once, and could hear a baby crying five floors away. She had the quick movements and nervous energy of a Hyde Park squirrel (which she called *squiddles)*, and like them she lived on a diet of fruit and nuts and root vegetables, which she would wash down with half a dozen cups of black coffee a day. She was addicted to high drama of any kind, and was easily capable of creating a commotion of her own invention if things began to get boring around the house.

Her favorite trick was one that she must have learned from the *squiddles* in the park. She would hide some little item that was important to us, and then stand back and watch our initial bewilderment slowly develop from concern to general panic. When at last the highly-charged atmosphere dissipated to the point where the targeted individual finally decided to replace the object or simply get along without it, Josy would suddenly find it under a bed or behind a chest of drawers and present it to her victim, who would be overcome with relief and gratitude. Josy Triumphant! She would then become the undisputed center of attention for hours on end as we all discussed the wonders of her eagle eye and her admirable generosity in spending so much of her valuable time searching for our things. It took us years to figure out what *that* was all about.

In early January of 1946 we began to notice that we had mysteriously developed the uncanny ability to keep track of our things with rather astonishing success. The birth of baby Heather had put an abrupt end to Josy's exasperating games, for the new arrival now occupied her full attention. She hovered over the baby day in and day out, dutifully attending to her every need before Heather was even aware that she *had* any needs. If she opened her mouth to yawn, Josy would fill it with sweetened apricot purée. If she wrinkled her face to cry, Josy would snatch her up and dance around the room with her, pushing the loudly whirring vacuum cleaner with her free hand to drown out the baby's memory of whatever it was that had made her want to cry.

At first we were grateful to baby Heather for keeping Josy busy fulfilling her many needs, but in time we began to realize that the situation carried hidden consequences for us. Now that Heather was a toddler she was free to explore our bedrooms while we were at school. If she happened to come across something of ours that she wanted, Josy would snatch it up and give it to her, drowning out our protestations with her new battle cry: *Let Heather have it!* Heather grew up in the firm and unshakable belief that anything belonging to us could be commandeered by her at will. It was no longer a question of "losing" our things and having them "found" and returned to us by Josy Triumphant. Now when we lost our things it was because they had ended up forever in the secure possession of Heather Triumphant.

The tantrum became Heather's weapon of choice. If we ever refused to let her have her own way, she would fill the house with ear-splitting wails that were topped only by Josy as she loudly demanded that we let Heather have it. Josy and Heather had teamed up together to become an unbeatable force, and we quickly learned that resistance was futile. The Borg had moved into 49 Charles Street.

Nothing is more infuriating to land owners or to the natives of a particular country or territory than to be forced to make room for uninvited immigrants or unwanted newcomers. Such invasions of privacy and property usually lead to bitter court cases or declarations of war. So it came as no surprise when my sister Wilda rose up in arms when she was asked to make room for three equally uninvited, unwelcome strangers who also happened to be her older siblings.

My mother, who had studied psychology in college, had taken great pains to prepare Wilda for our arrival. She knew that Sheila and Craig would not be a serious issue, since they were considerably older than the rest of us and were fully occupied with their own interests and pursuits. Craig was away all day at the Westminster School, and Sheila was busy

studying the stars and doing her needlework. But Wilda was
only fifteen months younger than I was, so the rumblings of
war could be heard in the land before I even arrived on the
scene. My mother did her best to dispel the looming thunder
clouds.

"Soon you will have a lovely new older sister," she said
in hearty tones to her skeptical child. "You must be very nice
to her and help her to feel at home. Remember, you've been
very lucky. You've had a mummy and a daddy all along, but
your sister Sonia doesn't know what that's like. She was too
young to remember us when she left home."

There's something about a hearty tone in a parent that
inevitably plants suspicion in the mind of a child, and Wilda
was nobody's fool. She could see immediately that my mom
was nervous about the reception she'd give me, and that only
served to arouse her curiosity. Why was she being asked to
share her bedroom with this unknown sibling? Why should
she be the one to have to give up a part of her space? Why
couldn't this lovely new older sister just come for a visit and
then go away afterward? Looking back on it all, I can't say
that I blame Wilda for feeling as she did. She would not have
been the only one in the history of the world to dream about
driving unwanted newcomers right into the sea.

"Your sister will need your help," my mother told her.
"She's had a very difficult time, far away from home. In fact,
she's never really *had* a home. Not the sort with a mummy
and daddy, anyway. So I want you to be the kind hostess,
and treat her as an honored guest."

But Wilda understandably balked at the idea of playing
the kind hostess to an older sister who had been parachuted
into the family without her consent and had already usurped
her position as the older child. Not only that, I was getting a
good deal of the attention that used to be lavished on her, and
that must have struck her as supremely unfair. And to top it
all off, I had been given half of her bedroom. Then, to add
insult to injury, my mother had asked her to be *nice* to me!

But the final blow for Wilda must have been having a sister who referred to her mother as *"my* mother."

Now, imagine my mother in a situation like this. Three Americanized children show up one day and are introduced for the first time to two little British children who don't quite know what to make of them, despite the fact that my mother spent a lot of time trying to prepare them psychologically for our arrival. She thought they had understood her careful explanations about the war and the forced separation and the upcoming reunion, but the reality proved to be very different from the stories she had told them about what it would be like to have us living with them. No matter how well you try to prepare children for a drastic change in the organization of a family, it seems that there are always unforeseen problems, many of which appear to be insurmountable. Not everybody can make it work as well as the Brady Bunch did, especially when the entire group of children has one trait in common: a strong sense of "self" and uncompromising personalities.

I'm afraid the worst clash of the Titans erupted between Wilda and me. Not only was Wilda (who was only six when I arrived) being asked to show a maturity well beyond her years in accepting me gracefully into her life, but the two of us were born with completely conflicting views of what a bedroom should look like. To put it bluntly, I wanted order and Wilda wanted chaos, and we feel exactly the same way to this day. This is why I'm utterly convinced that we were born with those differing perspectives. It's the sort of thing that's hard-wired into the genes at conception and can't be changed without the full benefit of gene therapy, which, of course, was as unavailable then as it is now. In fact, the gene had not yet even been discovered back then.

At any rate, the appearance of our bedroom became the greatest source of aggravation for both of us. I wanted all our things to be neatly arranged, with our clothes folded and put away in drawers. Perhaps I had learned this from Sheila, or maybe I simply inherited some of the same characteristics as she had, I can't say. All I know is that Wilda preferred the chaotic look of a bedroom strewn with her ill-cared-for belongings. If I asked her to clean up her stuff, she reminded me that I wasn't her mother. If I gathered it up in armloads and dumped it into her dresser drawers, it would be out again within minutes. If I'd been Sheila, I'd have been bouncing off the walls.

Wilda always claimed later that *I* was the one who drove *her* crazy by being such a neat freak, and I have no doubt that I did. Many years later I heard her telling Heather that I had put a strip of masking tape down the middle of the room, and I'd kick her stuff over to *her* side of the tape with the same athletic prowess and unbridled enthusiasm as a football player making a field goal.

I had to laugh at that one. Wilda did have her charm and an irresistible sense of humor. And she had a point, anyway. I must have been a thorn in her side, barging into her life that way and sharing her bedroom and all. My well-placed field goals turned out to be a temporary solution for me, but they were clearly an irritation for Wilda. We can look back on it now and laugh, but the endless frustration of not having our bedroom the way we wanted it might have led to an all-out war if I hadn't inadvertently come up with the solution. I had stumbled on a hobby that kept me out of the bedroom except for when it was time to sleep, and by then I was too tired to care any more about its appearance.

It all began when I developed an interest in constructing model airplanes. I discovered, to my immense delight, that they satisfied my perfectionist nature on the deepest level, and went a long way to counterbalancing Wilda's propensity for using our bedroom as an experiment in chaos theory. My mom came home one day with the model airplane kit that I had asked for, and I spent weeks in my father's study putting it together while he was in Paris.

I was thrilled with the results. It was a B-17G fighter plane, the best of all the B17's that had ever been built. It had chin, dorsal, ventral, and tail turrets, each mounted with a pair of .50 caliber machine guns. There were also left and right side guns in the cheeks and waist, and a single, rear-firing gun on the fuselage, making thirteen guns altogether. The plane had four engines, which gave the Germans what they called *vier motor schreck* (four-engine fear).

When I had finally finished making the delicate framework out of the long, thin, flexible pieces of balsa wood that came in the kit, I covered the whole thing with Japanese tissue, then painted it and stuck on the decals. The model airplane gave me a sense of accomplishment and a feeling of satisfaction that I had never experienced before, and I was on top of the world. Maybe it wasn't so bad to be a neat freak, after all.

My grandmother was horrified. She had been trying for a long time to dissuade me from becoming a tomboy, but she didn't understand the deep satisfaction my new hobby had given me. I loved making model airplanes, and it wasn't *my* fault that this appealed more to boys than to girls.

I almost had her convinced, then along came my dad and spoiled the beautiful impression of ladylike frilliness I had so carefully cultivated for her sake. He had bought us tickets to see Ethel Merman in *Annie Get Your Gun,* and I was blown away. It was the first musical I had ever seen in my life, and I identified with Annie right down the tips of her six-shooter guns. She wasn't a bit apologetic about shooting bull's eyes with hair-splitting accuracy, and people seemed to like her anyway, in spite of her tomboy ways. She was probably a neat freak too, I thought appreciatively. To me Annie Oakley represented everything a woman could be and should be, and this was a good fifteen years before women's liberation.

My grandmother was horrified all over again. My great interest in that "coarse" woman only proved to her that she had been right all along to be concerned about my worrisome inclination to engage in "male" pursuits. On top of that, I had taken to whistling the tunes from the musical.

Granny would shoot me disapproving looks as I walked by, and then recite her favorite warning:

A whistling girl and a crowing hen
will always come to some bad end.

Fortunately for me, I had no idea what she meant when she quoted those lines, other than to suggest that it wasn't ladylike for me to whistle around the house. But for me it made perfect sense to be a cowgirl and to ride horses and twirl my pistols and make model airplanes. These were *interesting* activities. I had spent long enough cooped up in the Trappist monastery at 46 Domingo Avenue, and now it was time to enter a new world of exciting adventure and challenging projects. My bemused parents encouraged me every step of the way.

Things continued to change for the better when I had a chance encounter with Nigel one day. He was sitting in his room playing quietly with his Meccano set (better known as an Erector set in America). I had disregarded him for the first few weeks of my tenure at 49 Charles Street, as he was four years younger than I was and therefore not a suitable play-mate for the knowledgeable and sophisticated girl that I considered myself to be. But there he was, playing with an *Erector* set! There had to be more to him than met the eye. Maybe I'd been wrong to overlook him that way. After all, Annie Oakley had a baby brother, and she sang about him very affectionately in *Annie Get Your Gun*. Some of the words popped into my head as I walked over to say hello.

My tiny baby brother can't even read a book,
Knows one sex from the other, all he hadda do was look.

"Hi, Nigel! My name is Sonia. I'm your big sister. Put 'er there, pardner!" I said, sticking out my hand.

"I know who you are," he replied, taking my hand and looking at me with huge, unblinking gray eyes.

"Who told you who I was?"

"Mummy."

"What did she say?"

"She said I should take care of you."

"*You* take care of *me?*" I laughed.

"Yes. I'm the man," he said simply.

"You're not a man yet, kid," I smiled, glancing quickly at his skinny little frame. I tried to imagine him dealing with the wicked witch in *Snow White,* which was the only scary movie I'd ever been allowed to see up to that time. I figured he was about the same size as the dwarfs.

"Say, tell me something, Nigel. Have you seen *Snow White?*" I asked him.

"Yes," he said, much to my surprise. He had already seen *Snow White* and he was only four! I wasn't allowed to see that movie till I was seven, when my father had come to Berkeley to bring us home. Craig had asked to see it on his personal special day.

"How come?" I asked.

"Wot?"

How come? was not a question that was well understood in the British Isles.

"How did you happen to see *Snow White?*"

"Walt Disney introduced me to her."

"No he didn't."

"Yes, he did. He invited us to a party. There were lots of children there, and we saw Snow White. She even gave us ginger biscuits. They were ever so good."

Now it was *my* turn to have eyes like saucers.

"You've got to be kidding!"

"What does *kidding* mean?"

"You're pulling my leg."

"No I'm not. I'm not even anywhere close to you."

"Nigel, listen to me. You shouldn't tell people that you know Walt Disney and he introduced you to Snow White. That's impossible. You might have gone to a party where someone got dressed up as Snow White, but you don't know Walt Disney. People don't dress up as Walt Disney, either."

"All right, then. But Daddy knows Walt Disney, and he introduced me to him at the party. He shook my hand, but I expect I can't really say that I actually *know* him. I can't say that I know you, either. Not yet, anyway."

"Wow! So you really *did* meet Walt Disney! Why does Dad know him? What does Dad do?"

"He's the Managing Director of Technicolor Films."

"Oh, yeah? What does that mean?"

"It means he's the man you go to see when you want to make a film in color. Walt Disney makes all his cartoons in Technicolor, and that's why they know each other."

"Oh, okay. So what did you do at the party? It must have been so exciting! What did you like best?"

"I liked the ginger biscuits best. They were jolly good."

Nigel and I spent the rest of the afternoon playing with his Meccano set, and we had the time of our lives. We had a few little problems understanding each other because of our accents, and our vocabulary was a little different too, but we soon sorted it all out. What I called a *wrench,* he called a *spanner,* and so on. We had just as much fun telling each other what all the new words meant as we did inserting bolts into the holes along the side of the oil rig we were building.

"What's Wilda like?" I asked him, as we worked along together.

"I don't know. She doesn't talk to me very much. But I think she's like a cross pixie."

"What on earth is a cross pixie?"

Crossword puzzles and cross-stitches and cross purposes did nothing to clarify the reference to cross pixies. I didn't yet realize that *cross* meant *mad* or *angry* in Great Britain.

"You know, like a pixie in the woods, sitting by a river and frowning because she's cross with everyone. Pixies look like Tinkerbell."

"Was Tinkerbell cross, then?" I asked him.

"Oh, yes. She used to get cross with Peter Pan when he didn't do what she wanted. Wilda gets cross with me too, when I don't do what she says. But I can't escape from her the way Peter Pan did from Tinkerbell. When she was mean to him he just flew away into the night. I wish I could do the same thing," he added wistfully.

"I wish I could, too. Wouldn't it be nice to fly away to Neverland and live there forever with the Lost Boys?"

"Yes. It would be very nice. I often think about that."

I realized then that my little brother had his problems, too. He had known isolation and loneliness in his own way, or he wouldn't have been thinking about Neverland with that special kind of yearning.

We talked about Neverland for a long time. We didn't want it to be a place where only children could live, though. We wanted it to have moms and dads who were always glad to see you and who couldn't wait to show you all the sights on the island in a small electric train or in an airplane with an open cockpit or in a boat that was commandeered by a one-legged pirate who knew how to be nice to children.

We had a wonderful conversation that afternoon. Nigel seemed to understand everything that mattered to me the most, including being Annie Oakley and riding off into the sunset on a spirited palomino horse.

"Did you like *Annie Get Your Gun,* too?" I asked him.

"Oh, rah-*ther!*" he said, enthusiastically. "I thought it was jolly good fun. We have the record, you know. Would you like to hear some of the songs?"

"What are you going to play the record *on?*"

"We'll play it on a gramophone, silly."

"A gramophone?"

"Yes. You put the record on a turntable, then you wind up the machine and you put the needle down on the record and you listen to the music. It's ever so much fun."

"I've never seen a gramophone before."

"Come along. I'll show you," he said, taking my hand.

We went to my father's study, and Nigel opened one of the mahogany cabinets along the wall. He pulled out a brown wooden box with a shiny brass trumpet on top, and set it on a nearby table. So this was a gramophone! It had a little decal on the side picturing a white dog with brown ears listening to his master's voice coming from the trumpet. Then Nigel went to the book shelf and took out an album containing a collection of 78rpm records featuring Ethel Merman singing songs from *Annie Get Your Gun.*

We spent the rest of the afternoon listening to the songs. Nigel knew most of them by heart, since he had heard the records so many times. I loved it when he sang along with David Manning, Ethel Merman's co-star, as he described how the girl that he married would have to be as soft and as pink as a nursery—the girl he called his own, would wear satin and laces and smell of cologne...

I remembered how Frank Butler had sung those words to Annie Oakley on the stage, and I pictured once again how she had looked as she listened to him. She had a sort of proud, hurt expression, as though she were disappointed in him because he didn't love her for who she was. Instead, he wanted her to look pink and lacey, and have a gardenia in her hair. I wondered how on earth a girl could lasso a little dogie (a *calf* in cowboy language) in that kind of a getup.

Just then the door opened and Josy came in.

"Oh, *there* you are!" she exclaimed. "I've been looking all over for you two children. It's tea time. Come along."

As we left my dad's study I saw my mom hovering near the door. She smiled happily at us as we passed her. I could tell by her expression that she had heard Nigel singing about the girl that he'd marry, but she said nothing about it. She was a very wise mum.

CHAPTER TWELVE

Two years passed without any major quarrels among the members of the English and American factions at 49 Charles Street. Nobody exploded at anyone else, and there were no cases of spontaneous combustion. We had all settled down into our various roles, the pecking order had been established, and each of us had our own lives to live, thanks partly to my mom's tireless efforts to find interesting things for us to do so that we'd be constantly busy and stay out of each other's hair.

Sheila had taken up weaving, Craig was in the fifth form at Westminster, Wilda spent hours on end drawing horses in her sketch pad, Heather had learned to walk and talk (with a little help from me), and Nigel and I had become fast friends, playing with his Meccano set, making model airplanes, and then crashing them with depressing regularity in Hyde Park. After the fifth crash we decided to switch over to model boats instead, which were less subject to violent accidents on the lake. They did, however, habitually get lost on the wide Serpentine, so we finally decided to sail them on a nearby pool where they could always find a safe haven against the rim on the opposite side.

We missed the American and Canadian soldiers who strolled around in the parks we frequented. Right after the war they used to give us chewing gum and candy, which we kept and treasured for as long as possible. These special treats were not available in the shops, so we were bowled over by their kindness and generosity in giving us such rare delicacies. They were probably homesick and yearning to see their own families again, so they were particularly friendly to us children, for perhaps we reminded them of their own kids. Some of them put us up on their shoulders, which made me think of how my father had done that too, when he came to get us in Berkeley.

It was funny, I thought, how the word "Berkeley" had followed me all the way to England, since our end of Charles Street connected with Berkeley Square (which the British pronounced *Barclay*). When our chauffeur, Thornley, was alone with us children in the car, he used to sing us a song about how a nightingale sang in Berkeley Square. He didn't really like singing alone, so he kept after us until we learned the words and sang along with him.

That certain night, the night we met,
There was magic abroad in the air.
There were angels dining at the Ritz,
And a nightingale sang in Berkeley Square.

What with Nigel and the gramophone and Thornley in the car, I did a lot of singing in postwar London. I found that singing made me feel happy, no matter what was going on at the time. Ever since those days I've always loved dinner parties where we gather around the piano afterwards and sing old-time favorites. Another song that Thornley used to belt out was about the teddy bears' picnic.

When you go down to the woods today
You're in for a big surprise.
When you go down to the woods today
You'd better go in disguise.
For every bear that ever there was
Is gathered there for certain because
Today's the day the teddy bears have their picnic.

When I think about Thornley I remember him with the greatest possible affection. He was always cheerful, always dependable, and seemed to love life with a childlike joy that exactly matched our own. I imagine that's why we liked singing together so much. The songs would raise our spirits as he drove us to school in the morning, and they'd lift our spirits again on the way home, where a lovely tea awaited us with watercress sandwiches or sausages and mashed potatoes or maybe, if we were very lucky, American hamburgers with ketchup.

This only happened when my father had just come home from one of his trips to America. It would amuse him to go through customs with a bottle of ketchup and a package of hamburger buns in his briefcase. It used to puzzle and worry the customs officers, who'd go into a back room to discuss it while my father chuckled behind his hand. He used to enjoy any kind of a situation that was a bit out of the ordinary, or that caused people to scratch their heads. He was always particularly fond of irony or whimsy.

Once, back in the days when Wilda and I were at war with each other on a continual basis, my mother would try to discuss with him what could be done to help us let off steam in a positive, non-violent way. My father knew that I loved Annie Oakley, so on one of his previous trips he had brought me back a cowboy costume with a ten gallon hat and two six shooter guns in holsters hanging from a belt with a big silver buckle. That was one of my favorite Christmas presents of all time. So after his conversation with my mother about our never-ending fights, my father brought Wilda a Christmas present, too. It was a Comanche warrior costume.

"Wilda the wild Indian!" my father chuckled. "Now you two girls can work off all your extra energy."

On the surface it appeared to be an amusing way of providing Wilda with an opportunity to express her hostility in a game-like, this-is-all-in-fun manner, but unfortunately for me her costume came with a bow and a set of suction-cup arrows, which she gleefully shot at me every chance she got. My only recourse was to shoot back with my cap pistols. It was Wilda Triumphant from then on.

Once again my mother came to the rescue. She was a past master at the art of working out how to schedule her war-like children to be posted in different places throughout the day, so that our paths crossed as little as possible. When we did have to be together she saw to it that it occurred in a family context with plenty of other people around to lower the tensions.

It was thanks to the need for this type of calculation on her part that I ended up as a student at the Cone School. The idea was to keep me occupied for five hours every afternoon in a very rigorous ballet program, with the expectation that I would return home too tired to fight with Wilda.

It worked exactly according to plan. We students would spend every morning doing academic work, then we would dance our little hearts out all afternoon. Evenings were spent doing prep (homework) for the next day. I hardly ever saw Wilda again until we moved to America, but that was several years later, and by then our mutual resentment had died a natural death. Good old Mum. She was a brilliant strategist. She had to be, to manage a large, high-strung family like ours.

The Cone School was founded by Grace Cone and Olive Ripman who, along with Miss Valerie and Miss Lily (Miss Grace's sisters), were our ballet mistresses for the highly-regarded ballet program. Today it is known as The Arts Educational Schools, located in Chiswick, London, and Andrew Lloyd Webber is the vice president.

But back in the postwar days the school was housed in a bombed-out building not far from where we lived (it later became the Canadian Embassy). A large part of the premises was condemned and out-of-bounds for us students. There was also no heat in the building, so in the wintertime we got chilblains which caused our feet to swell with an itchy sort of pain, a condition which made it hard for us to put on our ballet slippers in the afternoon. No matter. The British stiff upper lip prevailed, and we danced in spite of the chilblains.

After several years of rigorous training I won second place in the lower school dance program and was therefore allowed to participate in a command performance for the Queen of England at the Royal Albert Hall. It was just a small part and lasted only about five minutes, but it was a very exciting five minutes in my eleven-year-old mind. I rehearsed for many weeks under the vigilant eye of Miss Lily, who was my ballet mistress that year. Everything went well and according to plan, but I was disappointed not to see the Queen that evening. She was said to have been sitting in her box, but she wasn't visible to any of us dancers who were craning our necks from the wings. Ah, well. We knew she was there, and that was all that really mattered.

Come to think of it, I had one more close brush with the Queen before we moved to America. My aunt Stella Marks was a prominent portrait painter and miniaturist in London in those days, and she'd done some very fine portraits of my mother, my father, and Nigel that hung on the walls in our dining room. It was my mother's intention to have Aunt Stella do portraits of all her children so that we could join the rest of the family on the dining room wall.

I was chosen to be the next in line, so Thornley would drive me to my sittings at her studio while we both sang in loud voices along the way. My aunt Stella was serious about her work, however, so very few words were exchanged while I sat for her. She had to remind me not to move and to keep my eyes focused on a certain spot, but she was really very patient with my fidgeting and my wandering eyes.

During the fifth or sixth sitting there came a knock on the front door. Aunt Stella looked at me quizzically, then she shrugged and went over to open it. There was a murmured exchange, but I couldn't hear what they were saying. She returned shortly afterward with a man in a black suit trailing behind, and they both closed themselves into a back room. Minutes went by, then they both reappeared. The man looked totally composed, but Aunt Stella was flushed and rather excited, it seemed to me. She led him to the door, exchanged a few more murmurs with him, and closed the door quietly behind him. Then she picked up her paint brush and went back to work as though nothing had happened.

"Oh, I just can't *stand* it," she said a few minutes later, sticking her paint brush back into the jar of turpentine. "I have to tell *somebody,* or I'll absolutely *burst!*"

I peered at her out of the corner of my eye, wondering if it was okay to stop looking at the certain spot.

"Are you good at keeping secrets?" she asked.

"I think so," I said, trying to remember if I had ever kept a secret before.

"Can you promise me that you won't tell *anyone?* Not your mother, or your father, not your brothers or sisters, not even your best friend, or anyone else in the world? Think carefully now. It's very important."

I thought as carefully as I could, but I was unable to come up with any reason why I couldn't be trusted to keep a secret. Besides, I was so curious by then that I would have promised to keep a secret for the Queen of England herself.

"I promise," I said, deciding that it should be all right for me to take my eye off the certain spot.

"All right. I'm going to tell you then," Aunt Stella said, with a sort of desperate look. "I'm going to have to trust you, that's all."

She gazed at me speculatively for a few moments. I just sat there, trying to look as trustworthy as possible.

"That gentleman you just saw," she said finally, "he was a messenger sent by the Queen."

I drew in my breath. I had just been thinking about the Queen! How could that be?

"She's invited me to paint some portraits and miniatures for the Royal Family. That's why that man was here. He gave me her message, and now I must give him an answer. I must do it quickly, for you can't keep the Queen waiting."

"Well, accept the invitation, then! You'll be *famous!*"

"Not exactly," Aunt Stella replied. "The royal family prefers not to have publicity associated with their portrait artists. They don't want their name to be used in any negotiations or bargaining on my part to persuade future clients to give me higher prices, and that sort of thing. It would be sordid. You can understand that, can't you?"

"I think so."

"Anyway, the main point is that they want to handle the publicity themselves, making press releases at their own time and in their own way. It would never do for a little girl to spill the beans before they have a chance to make a formal announcement. Do you see what I mean?"

"Yes. I promise I'll keep it a secret."

"Good girl. So what should I do? Do you think I should accept their offer?"

"Of course!"

"Well, I'll certainly have to give it a lot of thought. It's a terribly important decision."

"Will you be allowed to finish the portrait you're doing of me right now?" I asked her. "Or will you have to run off to Balmoral or Windsor Castle or Buckingham Palace and start painting portraits immediately?"

"No, no, nothing like that," she laughed. "Don't worry. Your portrait will end up in your dining room, but I'm afraid the rest of you children won't be quite so fortunate. I'll be very busy from now on if I accept this commission."

When Thornley came to collect me that afternoon, I really did feel as though I were being "collected" rather than being "picked up" from my aunt's studio. My thoughts and feelings were scattered all over the place, and I couldn't even discuss it with Thornley. The agony of keeping a secret was just beginning, but he didn't notice a thing. He did make me sing with him all the way home, though, and that helped to make me feel better.

In the end my aunt accepted the invitation, and I kept it a secret just as I had promised. At first I felt very important and special because I was guarding a secret for the Queen of England. But it slowly began to dawn on me that it wasn't much fun to be the only one who knew how special I was. My aunt knew, of course, but she was just one person. Every once in a while we'd get together and wink, but that didn't amount to very much.

Then it finally occurred to me that she was showing me how to be brave in the face of temptation, for after all it must have been harder for *her* to keep the secret than it was for me, for *she* was the one, after all, who was going to be doing the royal portraits. She had chosen honor over fame, and I really admired her for that.

It took me a whole week to figure out that I had done the same thing. I had chosen honor over fame when I agreed to keep a secret for the Queen of England, but I couldn't tell anyone. At least not until they released the news to the press, and who knew when *that* would be? For a child of eleven, it seemed like forever.

CHAPTER THIRTEEN

Our favorite time of the day in London was in the late afternoon, when we would all go to Dad's study after tea and gather around Mum for some sweets (as they call *candy* in England). Dad was never there, of course. If he was in London at all he would be at the office until our bedtime, then he'd come in and say goodnight to us before going downstairs to have dinner with Mum, Granny, Sheila, and Craig, who were old enough to be allowed to eat dinner in the dining room (especially Granny). Nigel and I would be there too, but only in the form of our portraits on the wall.

Usually Dad was not in London, he was in his far-flung offices in Paris, Rome, New York, and Beverly Hills. So whenever he came home from his travels he would bring us all kinds of sweets from these different places, and Mum would dole them out to us in the study after tea. We liked chocolates most of all, and milk chocolate especially.

One day when we were happily munching away on our chocolates in Dad's study in the early spring of 1950, Mum suddenly announced that she had something very important to tell us. We all looked up at her expectantly, wondering what she was going to say. I hoped it wouldn't be a secret—it was hard enough guarding Aunt Stella's secret as it was.

"Next month," she began, "next month we're going on an exciting ocean voyage on the *Queen Elizabeth*. You're going to *love* the *Queen Elizabeth*. There'll be lots of other children to play with, and plenty of things to do."

Wilda jumped up off the floor and began dancing around the study, singing *"We're going on a cruise, we're going on a cruise, hey ho the merry-o, we're going on a cruise!"*

I just sat there on the floor, thinking how strange it was that Queen Elizabeth was always showing up in my life.

"What about school?" Nigel wanted to know.

"Don't worry about that," my mother smiled. "I have it all figured out. I've already spoken to your teachers, and they understand."

"Will we have to take prep with us?" I asked.

"No, that won't be necessary."

"We'll be jolly far behind when we get back, then, if we don't do our prep every day," I said, feeling rather worried.

"Well, that's just it. We're not coming back," Mum said in a matter-of-fact tone of voice, as though going on a cruise and never coming home again were the most natural thing in the world.

"Where are we going to live, then?" Nigel asked.

"We're going to Greenwich, Connecticut. It's near New York. We've rented a house just outside of town, on Round Hill Road. It's owned by a woman called Adele Simpson. She's a famous fashion designer."

"Is she going to live with us, too?" Wilda asked.

"No, she's going away for a whole year. She has another house somewhere else. But she's leaving her dogs with us to take care of. They're very friendly, well-trained negwooties —she told me so. You're going to *love* her house. You'll each have your own bedroom, except for So and Willie, of course. You two will be together."

"*Of course*," I thought, bitterly.

"There's a swimming pool," she added hastily, wanting to distract me from thinking too hard about sharing a room with Wilda again. "And there's a lake with fish in it and an island in the middle. And there's a dock with two rowboats. The whole property is surrounded by woods. You children will have a *marvelous* time."

"So are we coming back to London after Adele Simpson moves into her house again? Are we just going to stay for a year?" I asked.

"No, darling. We're never coming back. We're moving to *America!*"

There was that hearty tone again, which always raises a red flag where children are concerned. I knew right away that Mum wanted to convince us that America was better than England, but I had already lived there and I knew it was a place that had people like Miss Ava and Dick Egan living in it. Although our ballet mistresses were strict, they weren't cold and mean like Miss Ava, and I had never met a bully like Dick Egan at the Cone School.

"So where are we going to live when that lady wants her house back?" Nigel asked.

"Well, during the year that we live in her house, we're going to be looking for a house of our own. We'll look at lots of houses, then we'll buy the one we like best. You kids can help me make the decision. We'll have a *grand* time!"

"What if we don't find a house?" Nigel persisted.

"Oh, I don't see how that could possibly happen. A year is plenty of time to find a new house."

"What are the dogs' names?" Heather wanted to know. She was four years old by then, and had been begging for a dog for a long time. My mother, however, had stuck to her guns about not wanting to keep a dog in the city, so *Let Heather have it!* didn't cut the mustard with her.

"I don't know, dear. We'll have to ask Mrs. Simpson. Or else maybe you could name them yourself. I'm sure she wouldn't mind what you called them while she was away."

Heather's face shone with excitement at the thought of being the one who got to name the dogs.

"Do they have a ballet school in Greenwich?" I asked.

"I've already looked into that, So dear. There's a retired ballet dancer who lives in Greenwich, and she comes highly recommended. I've already been in touch with her. Her name is Madame Tarrasova, and she teaches ballet in New York City. But she lives in Greenwich and has a studio there as well, and she said she'd be delighted to have you join her little group. She was very impressed that you studied at the Cone School. She said she didn't need anything more than that as a recommendation for accepting you. So you're in!"

I could see that my mother was doing her best to sell us on the idea of moving to America. But why was she so eager to change our lives like that, right out of the blue? She must have been thinking about it for a long time, without saying anything.

"Now children, I want you to promise me you won't tell anybody about what I just said about moving to America."

Uh oh. More promises! I hoped this would be the last one. I wasn't sure how many I could hold in my head all at the same time. I didn't want to get confused and have to keep it a secret that Aunt Stella was moving to America, and that Mum, who was a very good artist in her own right, was going to paint portraits of the Royal Family.

"I want you to be sure not to say anything to Thornley," my mother warned us. "Especially *Mrs.* Thornley. She has a lot of friends in this neighborhood, and I wouldn't want her going around spreading gossip."

Gossip? I had always thought *gossip* was a word for the horrid, uncomplimentary things people sometimes said about other people. I couldn't see how anyone could find anything mean to say about our move to America. Everybody knows it's the land of opportunity, so why wouldn't we want to go? Maybe Mom was afraid they'd say something spiteful or envious like, "Well! How *nice* for them that they can afford to move to America. I wouldn't mind going there myself, but of course *my* husband can't even afford to take me to the cinema more than twice a year."

I soon found out what Mum was worried about. One of us eventually spilled the beans to Mrs. Thornley. The very next day they gave their notice, and within two weeks they had taken another position with a family around the corner on Curzon Street. Josy had to do all the cooking from then on, as well as her usual housework and child care.

My mother wasn't at all happy about any of this, but all she said was that children could be so unsatisfactory at times. It was hard for her to understand, she said, why children had such a difficult time keeping secrets when it would be so easy for us just to keep our mouths shut when we were asked to do so. She spoke to all of us at once, as though we had *all* run to Mrs. Thornley and said, "One, two, three!" and then spilled the beans all together in a chorus. I didn't like being lumped in with the rest like that, especially since I'd already proven that I could keep a secret. But nobody knew that.

In retrospect I came to understand my mother's decision to move us all to America. She was an American herself, after all, and in many ways she probably missed being with people who understood her and shared many of the same interests and opinions. It wasn't that she was provincial and needed the company of people who saw things in exactly the same way as she did. Quite the contrary, she loved traveling and getting to know people of other cultures. When she was in Japan with my father during the first two years of their marriage, she studied Japanese the whole time and took a course on the Japanese tea ceremony.

"And do you know how long your mother spent learning how to pour tea?" my father asked us one day. "That course was six months long. Can you imagine! It took your mother *six months* to learn how to pour tea. They take these things very seriously in Japan."

My mom had also spent two years filling a sketch pad with pen-and-ink drawings of the Japanese landscape, both physical and cultural, that demonstrated a very keen eye for interesting and humorous detail. She found the Japanese to be a delightful, amusing, and friendly people. Reticent, yes, and sometimes inscrutable, but always thoughtful, respectful, and generous hosts.

But during her years in England, on the other hand, the British made no bones about the poor opinion they had of her and her native land. She was from the colonies, they pointed out with the utmost disdain, so they immediately classified her as an uncultured boor. My mother was too polite and dignified to attempt to modify the preconceived notions that her detractors held so dear, but she couldn't help marveling at *their* boorishness in basing their opinion of her on such superficial and clearly ignorant generalizations. This attitude did not apply to all the British, of course, but she had been treated with scorn and disparagement by enough snobs to make them an undisputed factor in her decision to move back to the United States.

The main issue, however, was my father and his roving eye. He had been the perfect husband during their two years in Japan—attentive, romantic, and thoroughly entertaining. But when they moved to England the excitement of living in the inscrutable East was soon replaced by a life that was so routine and familiar to him that he quickly became bored and began looking for stimulation in the flattering, come-hither glances of beautiful women. These were not just one-night stands with women of so-called easy virtue. They were full-blown affairs with intelligent, accomplished women with whom my father believed himself to be deeply in love. These affairs would generally last for about three years or so: the first few months for the conquest, the next year-and-a-half for the glorious fulfillment, and the third year for gently extricating himself from a relationship that had inevitably grown tedious and overly demanding.

Obviously the first couple of years of the affair would be very hard on my mother. She felt undervalued, overlooked, and humiliated, not to mention murderously angry, and the contemptuous snobs who made up her coterie of so-called friends were of absolutely no help at all in her time of need.

"What can you expect?" they would say. "Kay Harrison is the sort of man who needs stimulation in his life."

The same was true of Granny, who felt no compunctions about reminding her that it was all turning out exactly as she had predicted. *She* could have handled Kay, she insinuated, but he was much too complicated and intelligent for Marion Belle to keep his interest. And this, coming from her mother as she reclined on the chaise longue at *her* expense!

I believe she eventually decided that since this highly unsatisfactory situation was not likely to improve, she might as well live in a part of the world that was more to her liking and where she could count on the comfort and support of faithful friends. It went without saying, of course, that she would feel much happier not having her husband's dalliances take place right under her nose. I imagine she hoped that he would find her more attractive, too, if she were not quite so available all the time. She was probably willing to travel any distance and be absent for as long as it took to encourage his heart to grow fonder.

Perhaps her strategy worked for a little while, but sooner or later it must have led to the out-of-sight-out-of-mind syndrome, for the truth of the matter was that once we were comfortably settled on American soil, we began to see less and less of him. Eventually we saw him only at Christmas. I often wondered if this was the outcome that my mother had expected all along, or if it was the result of a decision that had distanced her from him too much and for too long. Had she taken a gamble and lost?

Sometimes the most unlikely scenario turns out to be the one that is closest to the truth. When I look back on it now, I believe that she loved him enough to withdraw from the European arena and give him the freedom he needed to pursue his impossible dreams. As far as he was concerned, his soul mate had not yet materialized (except when he was in the first two stages of love), but he no doubt clung to the belief that some enchanted evening he would eventually see that desirable, long-awaited stranger across a crowded room. Meanwhile he was willing to climb every mountain, ford every stream, and follow every rainbow till he found his dream. He covered his sentimentality, of course, with a hard shell of caustic cynicism lest anyone ever suspect that he was really a closet romantic.

The words to *The Sound of Music* (which my father would later refer to as *The Sound of Mucus*) had not yet been written in 1950 when my mom made the decision to move back to America, but my dad lived by that credo even so. It was a little late in the century for romantics to be roaming the streets, for the Romantic period in art and literature had more or less died a natural death by the end of the nineteenth century. But romantics can never be fully trusted to be like everyone else. They pop up all over the place, whether or not there is a current Romantic Movement afoot, and they go where their hearts lead them no matter where that might be.

Don Quixote was a case in point. He wanted to live by the spirit of knight errantry even though the Age of Chivalry had died several centuries before his time. My father was yet another example of a displaced romantic operating totally out of context and about half a century after the Age of Romanticism had come to a close. Any comparison between a would-be knight errant with an impossible dream and a successful 20th century executive with highly realistic goals might seem like a bit of a stretch, but the comparison is less implausible when you probe the spirit that drove these two men, both romantics living in different time periods but motivated by the same yearning for what can't possibly exist in the real world.

Perhaps it's time to let my father speak for himself. Here is an excerpt from a letter he sent me on March 16th, 1954, when I was sixteen and he was a year short of sixty:

I would have you give much for the pulse of beauty and to cultivate your mind so that it might develop the wisdom to find the great ways of the world, the ways where the youth of your day would find the high qualities of life and the quest for perfection.

The older I become the more I realize that the meaning of life can only be understood from the experience of living intensely and being constantly aware of all its many prospects. To sharpen the mind by the quest for knowledge and to sweeten the heart by the touch of beauty — to seek and discover all that is lovely in this fantastic world — the urge to understand all the fine expression of the arts and so become aware of the high purpose of man.

There is a gold rim on the cup of your youth and I would have you drink deeply from it, for you could learn to be wise and tutor your mind to splendid things — in books, in poetry, in music, the arts of painting, sculpture, and the divine art of the dance — all of these things are there to be discovered.

Once aroused to their meaning, your life will sweep to high pleasures and beauty will adorn your brow and the great purpose of being in this world will support your progress along the highway to the stars.

Whenever I read his letters, I would end up in a state of near frenzy—my heart beating with the burning desire to drink deeply from the gold-rimmed cup of my youth, and to tutor my mind to the splendid things that awaited me in the world of art and literature. My father had planted the seed of romanticism in my highly receptive heart, and then removed himself to the mists of the mountain top where he would sit, guru-like, calling me in the dulcet tones of his siren voice.

My mother had responded to that call many years ago, and for a time the two of them must have enjoyed the first few steps of that inspiring journey together to the venerable Mount Fuji (*Fujisan*, as my mother used to call it), the mountain that had inspired so many artists and poets both in Japan and in the rest of the world.

But my mother had become Mrs. Kay Harrison, and had given birth to six children who, because of our young age, had inadvertently covered the snows of the lofty Mount Fuji with a patina of mundane, ordinary, everyday life. It's hard to follow the highway to the heavens when you can hear the distant cries of a baby who needs her nappies changed.

Don Quixote didn't have to worry about that. There would never be a Señora Quixote, for he had set his sights on an impossible woman—not one who was impossibly noble like the haughty ladies the troubadours craved, but one who was impossibly lowly—a hog farmer's daughter who was too practical and too realistic to entertain the notion of marrying outside her class, especially when the gentleman in question was crazy enough to think he was a knight errant and she was a princess. Thus she would remain forever true to the image Don Quixote formed of her in his imagination, with no danger of reality spoiling the impossible dream.

Kay Harrison, on the other hand, was a married man with six children, so my mother was doomed to failure when it came to keeping his cherished dreams forever shiny and elusive. It was inevitable that he turn his sights to other, more distant horizons, and my mother may very well have known that it was time to say farewell to him as he continued down the path of bright hopes and broken dreams. She either loved him deeply or she was just plain tired of it all, or both. All I knew was that I was rooting for both of them while at the same time I was nursing the secret fear that there was something shamefully ignoble about my dual loyalties.

"Will Daddy come with us to America?" Nigel asked, as we sat around my mother in the study.

There were no more chocolates left in the box. We had talked for such a long time that afternoon that they had been completely devoured without my mother even noticing.

"Of course he will, darling. You know he has an office in New York, which is very near Greenwich."

"You mean, he'll actually *live* with us there?"

"Not all the time, dear, but he'll be with us whenever he has work to do in New York. We'll see him just as much as we do here in London. He's always on the move, you know, traveling between his different offices, so it doesn't really matter where we live, as long as we're close to one of the places where he works."

Quicksilver, my mother thought sadly, as she pondered her husband's need to be forever on the go, and his uncanny ability never to allow himself to be trapped. She may have known very little about Don Quixote, but she did know what was driving her husband. She understood the poignant yearning for an ineffable place in the sun, for she felt it herself, and she felt it often. She respected the longing, the thirst, the ache, the deep nostalgia for something just barely perceived but never quite attained. Children understood it, and parents did too—you could tell by the catch in their voices as they sang lullabies about the land that lay just over the rainbow, way up high. Icarus understood the yearning, too (although he didn't live to tell the tale). But my mom couldn't risk falling to earth on molten wings—she had six children to worry about.

"Why can't we move to Juneau?" Wilda asked.

"Well fortunately for me, Technicolor has no offices in Alaska. It's much too cold up there. I just can't imagine how Primrose was able to put up with that climate."

But she did know—she just didn't know how to explain to small children what drives a man with a romantic nature to load himself down with heavy camera gear and trudge along wild and dangerous precipices in search of beauty so tender, so heartrendingly splendid that it stirs the soul to its very core. But it wasn't enough to perceive it—it also had to be expressed. The artist's deep-rooted need to communicate the ineffable was what drove Primrose forever onward, and his success was its own reward. Perhaps that's ultimately the story of every romantic soul.

Kay Harrison, my mother thought ruefully, was just as inventive and romantic as Percy Pond. That's probably what had attracted her to him in the first place, and it most likely also explained why we children had inherited a double dose of romanticism. But unlike Percy Pond, my father had chosen to dedicate himself to entrepreneurial pursuits, which is the hardest row to hoe for a man with deeply romantic inclinations. Only my mother could appreciate the creativity of his business dealings, but they weren't an obvious vehicle for artistic expression, like the photographs of Winter and Pond. Kay Harrison was a character in search of an author to articulate his yearning—only then would he feel that his dreams had been realized.

My mom could only hope that it wasn't already too late.

CHAPTER FOURTEEN

Our year at the "Simpson" house on Round Hill Road in Greenwich was like Pinocchio's candy island for us children, and its highlight was the swimming pool that sparkled invitingly in the morning sun. We'd gulp down our breakfast and gallop down the hill to this watery nirvana, where we would helplessly splash around in the shallow end, wondering how to master the mysterious art of swimming.

We needn't have worried. By the end of the summer we were as brown as nuts and swimming as well as the gracious frogs that were kind enough to share their pool with us.

The Simpson dogs turned out to be two poodles—one black and one brown—but without pompoms. Since Mrs. Simpson forgot to tell us their names, we decided to call them "Blackie" and "Brownie," but everyone pointed fingers at everybody else when my father came for a visit one day and immediately demanded to know which one of us had come up with such dreadfully unoriginal names. It came as a horrendous shock to him that any children of *his* could be so blatantly and unapologetically unimaginative.

I desperately wanted to please him by being as original as possible, but the harder I tried, the less creative I was. I toyed with the idea of wearing a beret like the artists who lived on the Left Bank in Paris, but it finally occurred to me that trying to develop a special, personal look was just about the most unoriginal thing I could possibly do. So I finally gave up and devoted myself to exploring the woods with Blackie and Brownie, who had no opinions about creativity one way or the other.

I learned, to my great surprise, that there was something about the woods that held a profound attraction for me. I went there every chance I got, much to the satisfaction of the poodles. I loved the smell of the woods, and the cool breeze, and the coziness provided by the lush trees and underbrush. Robert Frost was on our required reading list that summer at the Greenwich Academy, and I began to feel a true kinship with him.

The woods are lovely, dark, and deep,
but I have promises to keep,
and miles to go before I sleep,
and miles to go before I sleep.

I loved those words. They seemed deeply significant, even portentous. I was reminded of the day when I solemnly promised my aunt Stella that I would keep her secret for the Queen of England. How lovely it would be, I thought, to meander through these woods with the Queen. Maybe they would remind her of the woods near her castle in Balmoral, Scotland. We would walk in silence, both lost in our own thoughts, both knowing that we were sharing a secret that would bind us together for all the miles we would have to go before our final sleep.

I dreamed of living in a cabin in these woods that was just big enough for me and my favorite books and the two brave and adventurous poodles that were totally impervious to their lack of pompoms. I'd have a shelf where I'd keep a supply of all my favorite snacks: digestive biscuits and milk chocolate and candied ginger and marmalade and honey. Maybe I'd even be allowed to have a small potbellied stove so I could have hot chocolate and Horlick's malted milk all day long. I'd go home at night and feast on roast beef with Yorkshire pudding and green beans and gravy, but it would still be marvelous to have a little cabin to escape to during the day—a secret place where nobody would ever find me.

When you have so many brothers and sisters you begin to dream about log cabins.

One day when I was walking in the woods I found out what it means to be totally paralyzed with fear. Blackie and Brownie had gone charging ahead, their noses skimming the ground, and I was following along behind. I heard some dry autumn leaves crackling next to me, and I was surprised that the dogs had circled back without my noticing. Then all of a sudden I saw it—a huge black snake as thick as my arm, and so long that when I looked at its head I couldn't see its tail, it was so far away.

I literally froze. I wanted to run away, but I couldn't move. I felt as if I were in one of those dreams where you're trying to escape from a man who's chasing you but you can't —you're frozen in place. I thought for sure the snake would turn around and sink its fangs into me. I just knew I was a goner, and that nobody would find me till I was dead for at least three days. I was too paralyzed to even pant.

Eventually I began to realize that the snake was paying no attention to me at all. It just kept right on wending its way through the dry leaves, intent on reaching its own particular destination.

Little by little I started to thaw out, and soon I was able to breathe again. I ran straight home, with the dogs galloping on ahead of me, completely oblivious to my close encounter with certain death.

When I told Mom about the snake, she went to our set of encyclopedias and found out what it was.

"My goodness, you were right, So! It *is* a large snake! It's called a black snake, and they usually grow to be about eight feet long. They're known to be the biggest snakes in North America. The longest one on record was 101 inches. Just think of *that!*"

"A black snake? Is that what it's called? Just a black snake? Is that really its name?"

"Yes, that's what it says here in this article."

"Dad would have a *fit!* He'd want to know who decided to call it by such an unimaginative name!"

"It says here it's not poisonous," Mom continued. "It's a constrictor, and it likes to eat mice and rats. That's good. We need snakes like that. But it likes squirrels and birdies, too, and bird eggs."

"Oh! The poor little things!"

"Listen to this! If you scare a black snake or corner it, it'll imitate a rattlesnake and make a buzzing sound with its tail. It might even bite you if you frighten it, but its bite is harmless."

That black snake became the topic of conversation at the dinner table for a long time afterward. We were fascinated by the idea of living in such close proximity to monstrous creatures like that, and we speculated endlessly about how many members they had in their families, and how many families there were out there in the woods. Heather listened to all this with eyes as big as saucers, declaring that she'd never be caught dead in the woods.

I told her it would be best for her to stay as far away from the woods as she possibly could.

Mom added some terrifying stories about tarantulas with thick, hairy legs and beady eyes arriving in Juneau on banana boats from Central America.

"They moved sluggishly because of the cold, and then they died a slow, lingering death," Mom told us. "At least, that's what my dad used to say."

"Percy never said any such thing," my grandmother declared. "What a topic of conversation for the dinner table! Where are your manners? I don't know why you encourage this kind of talk, Marion Belle. It makes me feel sick to my stomach."

I saw a glint in my mother's eye as she put a succulent piece of roast chicken into her mouth and began to chew it with a distinctly untroubled appetite. I was old enough by then to realize that my strict Victorian grandmother invited rebellion from all but the congenitally pusillanimous or the very young.

I was relieved when Josy volunteered to take Heather trick-or-treating for Halloween that year. At least it wouldn't be *my* job this time. My mother had bought her a fairy princess costume, complete with magic wand, so Josy couldn't resist showing her off to the people in the neighborhood. Wilda and Nigel and I were too old for that sort of thing, but we weren't too old to dream up some mischief of our own for the occasion.

It occurred to me that it would be great fun to stuff some of Nigel's old clothes with newspapers and make a dummy for the front entry of our house. Nigel thought it would be a good idea to go one better—why not lay the dummy face down on the side of the road and hide in the bushes to see what people would do? We soon found out.

A car came along the road and slowed down when its headlights hit the dummy. The three of us smiled and nudged one another as we sat hidden in the bushes. A woman in the passenger seat rolled down her window and peered at the dummy, but she didn't get out to investigate. Instead, the car pulled away and drove swiftly down the road.

We all looked at one another, puzzled.

"Why didn't she try to help?" Wilda asked.

"Maybe when she opened the window she could see that it was just a dummy," I suggested.

"No, that's impossible," Nigel said. "We did a great job with that dummy. It looks real to me."

"Maybe she thought it was an ambush, and the dummy wasn't really dead," Wilda said. "She was probably smart not to get too close."

We waited a few minutes, but no more cars came. Then suddenly we heard a police siren in the distance. A squad car approached with its lights flashing and its sirens whining, and came to a halt behind the dummy. Two officers jumped out of the car, each holding a flashlight. One of them kneeled down next to the "victim," and gingerly probed it.

"It's just a dummy," he said, looking up at his partner. "Some kids must think they're pretty funny."

"Throw the thing in the squad car, then," said the other officer. "We'll take it to headquarters and have someone check out the labels on the clothes. They'll probably find plenty of clues."

We looked at each other nervously.

"I betcha the kids are watching us right now," the first officer said. "Light up those bushes, Joe."

We were through. Dead ducks. We flattened ourselves on the ground and waited for the axe to fall.

Suddenly the car radio crackled and a voice yammered something into the night. We couldn't understand a word of it, but to the officers it was as clear as day. They both turned and ran back to the squad car and drove away, their lights flashing and their sirens wailing as they went.

We all looked at one another, not knowing what to say.

"Saved by the radio," Nigel yelled. "Yay!"

"Hey, let's get the dummy, quickly!" I shouted.

"You go first," said Wilda.

We scooped up the dummy and ran back to the house as fast as we could go. There was nobody in the hallway, so we took the dummy upstairs and disassembled him. Just as we got downstairs Josy came back from her outing with the fairy princess, who was now carrying a basketful of candy.

We made a big fuss about how cute she looked and how lucky she was to have made such a big haul. Nobody ever suspected that the Greenwich police had almost made a big haul of their own that night.

There's something about being partners in crime that knits together even the most ill-assorted siblings. From that night on Wilda and I seemed to get along a bit better than before. She even made a tiny effort to keep her side of the room a little neater, and I made an even tinier effort to be a bit more understanding about the whole thing. It was a fairly tentative truce, but we both felt pretty good about it.

It was just as well that we had come to an agreement on the issue of tidy versus messy, for the next year we moved into our new house in Belle Haven, and once again Wilda and I were assigned to the same bedroom. This time the house was big enough for us all to have our own bedrooms —there were twenty rooms and ten bedrooms altogether— but my mother wanted one for a guest bedroom, and two for Craig (a bedroom and a study), even though he was away at college by that time. Maybe she felt that Wilda and I could handle sharing the same bedroom now that we seemed to be getting along a wee bit better.

The house was really very beautiful. Apparently it had been shipped, brick by brick, all the way from Andalusia by a wealthy American businessman who had fallen deeply in love with a Spanish duchess. He was worried she might be homesick when he plucked her out of Spain and moved her to Greenwich, so he not only gave her an Andalusian house but he also surrounded it with typical Spanish landscaping, with high brick walls and mazes made of green hedges, and fountains and pools with lily pads, and a little cabaña where she could find refuge when she wanted to be alone with her thoughts about her family and her distant homeland.

I had never heard of anything quite so romantic in all my life. I explored every inch of the house and grounds, thinking all the time about the lonely duquesa and the man who loved her so much that he laid an Andalusian mansion at her feet. No wonder my father had bought that exotically beautiful property. It came with such a gripping, compelling tale that he probably couldn't resist.

But an interesting history does not a sensible dwelling make. Our new house was originally designed for the climate of southern Spain, where the winters are mild. But we had a freeze/thaw cycle all winter long in Greenwich, so it should have come as no surprise that the stucco cracked, the bricks leaked, and the heating and maintenance bills were sky high. My father's romantic personality would cause him, once in a while, to compete quite successfully with Percy Pond's own "absurdly impractical" nature.

Because of my father's chronic absenteeism, my mother was left with the responsibility of seeing to it that the house and grounds were properly maintained. She never dreamed that anything quite so mundane as a lawnmower breakdown would lead her to the perfect man for the job, but life can be unpredictable sometimes. In fact, it almost always is. So as my mother stared helplessly at the recalcitrant lawnmower standing obdurately by the property line abutting Otter Rock Drive, a passing pedestrian happened to glance at her over the low-cut hedge. When he saw she was a lady in distress, he paused and called out to her.

"Hello over there! Are you all right? Do you need some help?"

My mother looked at him bashfully and hesitated for a moment. He was dressed in jeans and a blue shirt, and was carrying a rake in his hand. He was darkly handsome, with a strong jaw, warm brown eyes, thick black hair, a straight nose with flared nostrils, and a sympathetic smile. Why, my mother wondered, were all handsome men inevitably tall and dark?

"Well, I suppose I do need a little help," she said finally. "It looks as though the motor on the lawnmower has given up the ghost."

The stranger threw his rake into the back of a nearby pick-up truck, then walked a few paces into the middle of the road and turned around to face her. Then, much to her great astonishment, he suddenly made a running leap right over the hedge, then strolled over to my mother with a confident, manly gait.

"Let's have a look," he said, bending over the machine. "Is that all right with you?"

"Oh, yes of course," my mother said, noticing an accent of some sort. It sounded Spanish to her, but she wasn't sure. He had a good command of English, so it was difficult to say what his native tongue might be.

The handsome stranger listened closely to the sputtering engine as he made several abortive attempts to start it up.

"When did you last clean the spark plugs?" he asked.

"Spark plugs?" my mother echoed.

He smiled and took a piece of sand paper out of his back pocket. Then he kneeled down on the grass and proceeded to rough up each of the spark plugs.

"There. That ought to do the trick!" he smiled, reaching for the ignition switch.

The engine suddenly burst into life and purred quietly while the stranger stood there grinning.

My mother was happy, relieved, impressed, grateful and nervously excited, all at the same time.

It turned out that his name was Emilio Romero, and he was from a good family in Argentina who had known better days. He had lived all his life on the pampas, and was an experienced gaucho and groundskeeper for his family's estate—exactly the kind of experience my mom was looking for, except, of course, for the equestrian talent, which was not really required in residential Belle Haven. At any rate, he was now working as an independent landscaper, and he was happy to find a place for my mother in his schedule. It was not long before the house and the grounds began to return to their former glory.

As time went by my mother began to develop a deep respect for Emilio's competence and artistic sensibilities. She loved his cheerful nature and good spirits, and looked forward to meeting with him in the morning to discuss the day's agenda. But she also sensed danger—not on the part of Emilio, necessarily, but certainly because of him. The danger lurked in her own heart, so she treated him with a formality that was meant to keep him well beyond arm's length, in a safe zone where she could deal with him in a businesslike, professional manner.

She took great pains to keep my grandmother in the dark as much as possible, knowing that she would loudly voice her opinions from the comfort of her chaise longue if she thought there was any impropriety in her dealings with the Spanish gardener, as Granny liked to call him. She had always been a fan of A.J. Cronin's novels.

My mother was worried right from the start that she might become something of a Croninesque figure herself, but she also sensed that there was very little she could do about the hopeful exuberance that was moving stealthily forward all on its own, like a character on the stage or in a novel, stepping inexorably along a flagstone path to a secret garden filled with promises that covered the high brick walls like a profusion of colorful spring flowers.

CHAPTER FIFTEEN

The French call it a *coup de foudre*—a lightning strike. Barely three weeks after meeting Emilio Romero, my mom was thinking about him full time, straight time, all the time. There was never a moment when he wasn't on her mind. There was never a minute when she didn't see his face, or at least try to see his face. She hadn't yet memorized every detail of his features well enough to see him perfectly when she tried to conjure him up in her mind, but she was close—very close. She still wasn't sure about the earlobes, or the angle of the nostrils, or the length of the sideburns, or the shape of the fingernails, mainly because when she did see him she could only glance at him briefly so that he wouldn't catch her staring.

Then one hot summer morning she decided to take him a glass of lemonade lest he get heat stroke while he clipped the hedges. That was when she saw him without his shirt. She gasped, yes *gasped* at the sight of him, just like the heroines of those romance novels. Her gasp had echoed around the mansions of Belle Haven, and every door had opened so that the neighbors could peer at her through their binoculars. At least, that's the way she felt. She stopped dead in her tracks, the once-cold glass of lemonade sizzling with the heat of her trembling hand.

No! She had to stop this nonsense at once. What would Kay think if he knew? He would be horrified by the kind of cheap purple prose that was running through her head. It was the sort of thing one found in *True Stories* magazine. She would live forever in disgrace if Kay guessed how she felt about the Spanish gardener.

My father was accustomed to being elevated to the very height of rapture by women of considerable accomplishment, however, so the female equivalent of my mom's Spanish gardener would never have made it to his pantheon of former mistresses, although he might have made an exception for a woman who worked in a cigar factory in Seville if she had been endowed with Carmen's irresistible attributes.

Generally speaking, however, his paramours stood out among their peers in European society for their noteworthy achievement in the arts. One was a highly-regarded prima ballerina with the Paris Opéra Ballet, while another was a well-known photographer whose work was in the Gallérie Condorcet, and yet another was a gifted sculptress who had once studied under Giacometti. The latest one, my mother thought with some satisfaction, was merely his secretary, but my dad had been quick to point out that her position was only temporary and purely circumstantial, for her real goal was to be a novelist, and he was sure she would succeed very well in her literary endeavors. She had yet to write a novel, but he had no doubt that it would soon be forthcoming.

Why, my mother wondered, could he not understand that he always sought the attentions of celebrities because he saw them as marks on his escutcheon? And why did he not realize that these women, who were unmarried or separated from their husbands, were in the market for a suitable male on whose arm they could be seen at the most exclusive social events of the season? Kay was a known wit and a raconteur, and could be counted upon to enliven any social gathering. Since he lived by himself in London and Paris, he was seen as fair game and was sought after by the season's best picks among the ladies. It seemed quite obvious to my mother that he was eschewing the thorny way to heaven in favor of happily treading the primrose path of dalliance, although to my father it was not a question of dalliance at all. For him it was all about living life to the hilt and reaching for the stars that lay well beyond the pearly gates of heaven, which to him was a place of unspeakable boredom that represented everything he disliked about pious mediocrity.

Be that as it may, my mother now had to take a careful look at her own heart. Did Cupid shoot his arrows at just any random person who happened to be in the way? What was it that made love real and true and deep, and not just some game involving well-marked escutcheons? What was it that she saw in Emilio Romero that had had such a profound and almost unseemly effect on her? She had been felled by love, like some silly teenager, after a lifetime of self-sacrifice and kept promises. She now found herself in virgin territory—fearful, worried, and alone, but filled to overflowing with excitement, hope, joy, and yearning.

"Oh, Mrs. Harrison, I'm glad you came," Emilio said as she approached him with the dripping glass of lemonade. "I wanted to ask you about these hedges. I could cut them into geometric shapes for you, if you like."

"Have you done any topiary before?" my mom asked him, intrigued by his suggestion. She kept her eyes glued to his face so as not to stare at his bare chest.

"I have," he smiled. "I used to be the *topiario* specialist on my father's estate in Argentina. Are you familiar with the etymology of this word?"

"No," my mother answered. "Tell me."

"It's Latin for a landscape gardener, or a *topiarius,* who is a designer of places, or *topia.* You see? If you stay close to me you can learn something new every day."

A landscape gardener talking to her about Latin words! What next? My mother gazed at him in fascination while the condensation from the lemonade ran down the inside of her arm. Emilio nodded his head toward the glass.

"Is that for me, by any chance?"

"Why yes," my mother said. "I thought you might be thirsty out here in all this heat."

"You're very kind," he said, accepting the glass.

"Don't mention it."

"But I can't drink this without sharing it with you," he added, offering her the glass. "Won't you have some first?"

"Well, I…"

"Go on, have a few sips. It's such a hot day."

"All right then," my mother said shyly. She took two or three swallows, then handed him the glass.

"Is that all you want?"

"Yes, I've had plenty. I really wanted *you* to have it."

"Thank you, then," he said, tipping his head back and thirstily draining the glass.

My mom took the opportunity to look at his chest while he drank the lemonade. He had a mat of black hair over his pectoral muscles, with a thin line running down the middle of his torso and into his trousers. She quickly looked back at his face as he lowered the empty glass and sighed with happy satisfaction.

"That was good," he said, with genuine appreciation. "You made it yourself with fresh lemons, didn't you?"

"That's right," my mom replied, with a touch of pride.

She told me all about her encounter with Emilio that night after dinner. Not every detail, of course—she supplied those little by little over the years, and I slowly put them all together as they came back to me. I particularly recall how impressed she was when Emilio told her he had seen some excellent examples of topiary elephants at the Royal Palace at Bang Pa-In in Thailand.

"He has such a good education and a very fine mind," my mother said, smiling happily at the very thought of him. "He's traveled all over the world. I never cease to be amazed at the interesting things he knows."

"Why did he leave Argentina, then?"

"Things didn't go well for the upper classes during the Perón government. His family ended up losing everything they had, so Emilio moved here to the States."

"Why is he only a gardener, then?" I asked. "Couldn't he have found a better job?"

"It can't be so easy, I suppose, coming to a new country and not speaking the language fluently. He says he's happy with his job, though. He's used to being outdoors. His family owned an *estancia* in Argentina, which is what we'd call a ranch. Anyway, he says he's learned to get along with a lot less than before, and he likes it that way. Life is much less complicated now."

"I like the sound of him," I smiled. "He seems down-to-earth and genuine."

"He is, you're absolutely right," my mother said, her eyes sparkling. "He has a happy-go-lucky, relaxed attitude to life, and that makes him very easy to be with."

"What about... well, does he have a wife?"

"They're separated, he told me. When he lost his fortune she went home to her father, but he didn't want to follow her there and be dependent on her family. So he decided to come here and start all over again. There's probably more to it than that, of course. There must be some other reasons why they separated, but I didn't want to pry."

"He must be lonely, though, so far away from home and not knowing anyone."

"Yes, I'm sure he is, but not because he doesn't know anyone. He has lots of pals at his pub in Portchester. He's a friendly, outgoing man. But his problem is that he hasn't had the opportunity to meet anyone around here who shares his background, and who is well traveled enough to understand his culture or speak his language."

My mother gave a sigh and looked thoughtful.

"I wish I knew how to speak Spanish," she said finally, with a wistful look in her eyes.

"Maybe Emilio will teach you," I said.

"Oh, I'm too old to learn a language now," she replied sadly. "I should have done that when I was young. But it never occurred to me to study languages in Alaska or in San Francisco either, for that matter. I never dreamed I'd have the chance to travel the world until Daddy came along. I did study Japanese in Japan, though, but that's about as far as I got. And I was young, then."

I was proud of my mom for being able to speak Japanese well enough to have conversations with astonished waiters in Japanese restaurants. She turned into a completely different person when she spoke Japanese—she became bashful and giggled behind her hand, just like any other Japanese woman of her day and age. I wondered if she'd become fiery and passionate if she learned to speak Spanish.

Some of my happiest childhood memories were of the Japanese dinner parties my mother would put on once in a while just for the family or for her special friends. She would spend all day with Josy in the kitchen, preparing *miso* soup and making all kinds of *sushi* such as *maki* (finely sliced raw fish or raw veggies and rice held together with dried seaweed called *nori),* and *nigiri* (clumps of hand-formed rice topped with sliced raw fish), and *inari,* (toppings stuffed into a small pouch of fried *tofu,* or fermented soy bean paste). What I liked best was the succulent *sashimi*, which was simply raw fish all by itself, undisguised by rice or seaweed or pouches of any kind. Just raw fish *au naturel.* My mother would arrange these colorful creations very artistically on lacquer fishing boats like the ones on the Tokyo Bay (the *Edo-mae*) during the *Edo* period that spanned the late 18th and early 19th centuries.

We sisters would dress up in our kimonos and put black wigs on our heads, with chopsticks sticking out of the buns on top. Then we made up our faces to look like our idea of geisha girls, with white face paint, black eye make-up, and bright red lipstick. Craig refused to make up his face to look like anybody at all, but Nigel had a *samurai* costume and a sword to go with it, which gave him permission to chase the poor geisha girls around the dining room with impunity. My father wanted to solve the problem by giving him a *kamikaze* outfit instead, but my mother wouldn't hear of it. She wasn't about to let her beautiful boy sit with the guests at the dinner table dressed up like someone who was intending to commit suicide in the morning.

"My cooking wasn't *that* bad," she smiled ruefully when she told the story.

Little did we know that it would be my grandmother, and not the kamikaze pilot, who would die the morning after one of my mother's Japanese dinner parties. It wasn't my mother's *sashimi* that killed her, though. Granny had complained of "feeling poorly" after the party, and had taken some Alka Seltzer to settle her tummy, as she put it. Later that evening she rang for Josy and asked her to call the doctor. The pain had gotten much worse, and she was afraid she might be having a heart attack.

When the doctor arrived at the house he took out his stethoscope and listened to my grandmother's heart, then he immediately called an ambulance. She was taken as quickly as possible to Greenwich Hospital, where a cardiologist was waiting to examine her. My mother and Nigel and I had followed the ambulance in the Rover, but by the time we got it parked and found Granny's room, the cardiologist had already finished his examination and was waiting to give us his diagnosis and prognosis.

"It doesn't look good, I'm afraid," he said. "I'm going to have to come straight to the point, as there isn't much time left. So I'll have to tell you, it doesn't look to me as though she's going to make it through the night. I'm very sorry. I'll prescribe some medication to make her comfortable. She won't suffer, don't worry. But really, she's done very well if you think about it, considering she's 87 years old. Her chart says that she hasn't ever had any other health problems."

I knew he was trying to get us to look on the bright side, but the fact that she hadn't had any other health problems seemed peripheral to the major one she was facing just then.

"I'm on duty tonight, so I'll be close by if you need me," he said. "Do you have any questions for me?"

We looked at one another and we looked back at him, but we couldn't think of anything to ask him. It all seemed so sudden and so final. How do you say goodbye to someone when you aren't prepared, when you have no idea it's going to have to be that very same night, when you least expect it, right after a heavenly Japanese dinner?

I suddenly realized that I still had my geisha make-up on, although I had remembered, thank goodness, to take off my kimono and my wig and put on a sweatshirt and a pair of jeans.

The doctor had been wonderful about it. He pretended that he hadn't noticed that a geisha girl was standing there in front of him, listening to him telling us that our grandmother wasn't going to make it through the night.

We sneaked into Granny's private room to see how she was doing. I don't know why we thought we had to be so quiet. This was probably the one time in her whole life that she didn't feel like sleeping, since she was fighting hard just to stay alive.

The lights were dimmed so we couldn't see her too well, but I could tell that she was propped up in bed, with tubes up her nose and an IV taped to her wrist. She didn't greet us or even look at us. In fact, she didn't seem to know that we had come into the room at all. Even if she had known, she might not have been able to see us in the semi darkness.

As we approached her bed I could see that her eyes were focused on the white wall in front of her, and they seemed to be wide with fright. She was staring at something that she evidently thought was terrifying. She was trying to scream, but no sound came from her lips except some feeble, deep-throated little warbling sounds that were more like pleading, half-hearted protests than anything else. What did she see on that blank wall?

I went to her bedside and called her name, but she didn't respond. She just kept on staring at the wall, still wanting to scream. Maybe she was having one of those dreams where you feel paralyzed and can't run away from an ugly, scary man who's chasing you. I didn't remember ever wanting to scream as I attempted to run away, but maybe if I had tried it would have sounded like what my grandmother was doing.

I suddenly remembered the "man" who had stood at my bedside in Berkeley, looking down at me with no expression on his face, no pity in his eyes, and no mercy in his heart. I had cried hard and loud because I was five years old and fully awake and totally terrified, so I was able to belt out my crying with ear-piercing conviction. Granny had rescued me then, and I wanted to rescue her now.

"Granny, you're having a bad dream," I said, leaning close to her ear. "That man you see by the wall, he's not really there. He's nobody, Granny. He's just a nightmare, that's all. You must drink a glass of water, then you'll be all right. Remember how you gave me a glass of water when the man came to visit me that night in Berkeley? The glass of water made everything much better."

My grandmother replied with another series of warbles. This time they seemed to be coming from deep inside her lungs, with fluid crackling every time she exhaled. I went and got her a cup of cold water from the bathroom sink. I tried to give it to her, but she wouldn't take it. She just kept staring at the wall, trying to scream.

"Mom, what can we do?" I asked her, feeling desperate.

"I'll go and talk to the nurses," she said. "Maybe there's something they can give her. An injection, or something."

"I'll go with you," Nigel said, a little too eagerly.

I stood by the door and watched them go down the hall. Then I turned back to my grandmother to see if there was anything else I could do to help her stop wanting to scream at whatever it was she was looking at on the wall.

I remembered how she had come to my bedroom that night when I was crying while the man stood there looking at me with scientific curiosity, as though I were some kind of an exotic insect and he had just stuck a pin through me so he could examine me while I struggled. Then I remembered that when he heard Granny coming up the stairs he had calmly set his legs so that he'd be ready to spring into action, then as soon as she turned on the light he flew horizontally out the window.

I reached over to the light switch by the door and flicked it on, and suddenly my grandmother's warbles and crackles stopped coming.

"We did it, Granny!" I cried triumphantly. "We made him go away! Did he fly out the window? Did you see him fly away?"

No answer.

"Granny?" I said, going over to her bed.

No answer.

When I got close to her I saw that her dark brown eyes were half open, looking at me with a glazed expression.

She was gone.

Just then Mom and Nigel came back with a nurse.

"This lady will give Granny something to help her feel better," Mom said, as she came through the doorway. She had that special hearty tone of voice that she used when she was trying to get us to believe something she couldn't really believe herself.

The nurse went over to the other side of the bed. She bent over my grandmother for a moment, and then turned to face Mom.

"I'm sorry, Mrs. Harrison," she said, in a tone of gloomy sympathy. "Your mother has passed away. I'm very sorry. I'll get the doctor."

She quickly left the room while the three of us stood by Granny's bed. As I peered at her face I noticed that she now looked calm and relaxed.

The man of darkness had been chased away by the light, and my grandmother was at peace.

CHAPTER SIXTEEN

Emilio was wonderful to my mother after Granny died. He was helpful, attentive, thoughtful, and considerate of her feelings during her period of mourning. He had been deeply troubled when his own mother had died, so he knew exactly how she felt about losing Granny. At least, he thought he did.

Mom didn't like to say anything to him about her mixed feelings. He seemed to have been so close to his own mother that she was afraid he'd be disappointed in her if he realized that she was relieved now that Granny would no longer be reclining on her chaise longue, telling her how to run her life. Worse still, he might think she was overly sensitive to have reacted bitterly to my grandmother's meddlesome, dictatorial nature. She already knew that men from Spanish cultural backgrounds tended to put their women on pedestals, and would take great umbrage at anyone who insulted them or was seen to criticize them in even the mildest way. So my mother was leery of saying anything in front of Emilio that suggested even the slightest disregard for Granny, especially now that she was dead.

But in many ways she felt the same way as Emilio did about his mother. When people die they inevitably leave a great hole in our lives, no matter what their faults might have been. So Mom struggled with a sense of guilt for not giving Granny enough credit where credit was due. Maybe she had overemphasized her unsatisfactory characteristics and paid too little attention to her many good qualities. Granny was a fighter—she had put up with severe discomfort in Alaska to keep the family together for as long as she could. She had worried constantly about Edwin's welfare in San Francisco, and she had worked hard as a single mother to support the family when she was forced to go to back to California for Edwin's sake. She was the very epitome of an all-American woman with a pioneer spirit and plenty of practical common sense, but she lacked subtlety, my mother thought. The more she thought about Granny, the more her mind would wander off in the direction of her perceived faults. She would sternly berate herself for this, but it was Emilio's disapproval that she feared most of all.

She needn't have worried. Emilio Romero was not an unsophisticated man—in fact, he was an excellent judge of character. He had observed my grandmother long enough to understand the battle that was going on in my mother's heart, and he fully understood my mother's reasons for wanting to make a good impression on him. He was both moved and flattered by her efforts in that regard, and he felt excited by the implications for their developing relationship.

For Emilio, too, had been hit by the *coup de foudre*. I have no way of knowing exactly what was going on in his heart, but I did notice the way he looked at my mom, and the care he took with his appearance, and how nervous he was when she was around. In the very beginning, when he first started working on the landscaping, he was open and hearty and sure of himself. But as time went by he became bashful to the point of being tongue-tied sometimes. My mother told me later that she had also been touched by these changes in his demeanor, and was just as excited by their implications. My mother and Emilio were falling in love, and they were fighting it with all their strength.

Mom once told me how Dad was always hoping for *his* knight in shining armor to come along and rescue him from his marital obligations. Most of the women in his life had wanted to become the next Mrs. Kay Harrison, an ambition that exasperated my mother. They, too, were incensed by her refusal to step aside and let them marry her husband.

So in spite of her love for Emilio and her desire for male companionship, my mom fought a brave battle to keep things "on the up and up," as she put it. Aside from wanting to do the right thing and be a faithful wife and a good role model for her children, she felt it was of paramount importance not to give my dad any legal reasons for seeking a divorce. Not only would she hate to make an honest woman out of one of his calculating paramours, but it would be terrible for Emilio to get involved in such an imbroglio. It was always possible, she thought bitterly, that my dad would name him in a law suit for alienation of affection. This would have been ironic indeed in the light of his own behavior, but he held the purse strings and he would therefore be able to afford a better lawyer.

It was just at about this time that Josy seized the chance to make a little mischief. She must have been struggling with feelings of jealousy and envy for many years, which might explain why she was always figuring out underhanded ways of getting control over the rest of us. She had developed a variety of methods that worked quite well. She'd use charm and flattery to get us to confide in her, then she'd go and tell other family members what we had said, which would turn us against one another. If we complained to her about what she had done, she would pretend to be completely innocent, claiming she had only been trying to be helpful. This would excuse her betrayal and at the same time it would make us feel guilty for not understanding her intentions or sufficiently appreciating her efforts on our behalf. Josy Triumphant!

My mother was the ideal victim for Josy this time, for her feelings for Emilio were so strong that she was unable to control her obvious enthusiasm, nervousness, distraction, and other symptoms of love. Josy watched these developments with narrowed, calculating eyes, waiting patiently for just the right opportunity to strike.

The moment arrived one afternoon when my mom took Emilio with her to Gristede's to help her with the groceries.

This was not the first time they had gone to the grocery store together, but on that particular morning they were sitting in the car, talking for a moment before getting out. Josy went to the car and opened the passenger door.

"Oh!" she exclaimed, putting her hand to her mouth. "I had no idea that you two were... I didn't mean to barge in on anything. I came to help Madam with the groceries. I didn't realize you were both in the car together. I'm so very sorry! Please excuse me."

Then she closed the passenger door and ran back to the house, acting flustered and embarrassed.

Two minutes later my mother came storming into the house, letting the door slam behind her.

"How dare you act as if you were interrupting something private that was going on in the car?" my mother said, with uncharacteristic anger.

"Well, I had no idea that Emilio and you were..." she pretended there were no words to describe what she saw.

"You're being *ridiculous!*" my mother said, raising her voice. "Emilio and I were discussing his work schedule for this afternoon."

"I see," said Josy, sounding unconvinced.

My mother felt the anger rising. The truth was that she had been enjoying that moment of quiet intimacy close to Emilio in the car. They had never lingered in the car before, so my mother was probably looking forward to reliving the moment many times in the days to come. Then Josy had to come along and spoil it.

What infuriated my mother most of all was the fact that she just *knew* that Josy had butted in on purpose to ruin the moment. Then what doubly infuriated her was that she was foolishly trying to correct Josy's opinion of what she had seen, when in fact she owed the woman no explanation at all. She knew that Josy had secretly sullied a precious moment and was smirking about it. She felt like killing her. What was worse, she knew that the more indignant she felt, the more satisfaction Josy would derive from the situation. And worst of all, this wasn't the first time that Josy had pulled a covert, underhanded stunt. How do you deal with a calculating, manipulative woman? Guerrilla warfare is the most difficult form of combat, with traps and hidden mines everywhere.

"Don't you ever go out to the car again when I'm talking with Emilio!" my mother almost shouted. "You're not to interrupt me. Ever! Do you hear?"

"My goodness," said Josy, lifting her hand to her bosom. "I had no idea your private conversations with Mr. Romero were *that* important to you. But don't worry. I'll never go *near* the car again. I just hope you won't have too much trouble carrying the groceries in when Mr. Romero isn't with you to help with the heavy bags."

"When Mr. Romero is with me, I won't need help," my mother said evenly. "When he's not with me, I'll need your assistance. That ought to be perfectly obvious."

"Of course, Madam. It's just that it's hard for me to see whether or not he's with you in a dark car, parked under the elm tree like that. But I'll do my best."

My mother stalked off to her room and sat heavily on the bed. She had not finished going over the schedule with Emilio, but now she was too angry to talk to him just then. She wouldn't have wanted him to see her in such a state. He probably wouldn't have understood, either, just what it was that aggravated her about Josy so much.

"It would have taken him years," she told me later, "to understand what a clever manipulator she was. She always seemed so *nice*, you know. People thought she was a lovely, delightful person. They never dreamed that underneath it all she was a controlling, calculating woman who had a lot of tricks up her sleeve when it came to getting her own way. And getting her own way meant being in the limelight and having power over other people. She was like Granny that way, but at least Granny was open and honest about bossing people around. She was never manipulative. You just did what she said, and that was that. Granny was the one with the most character, and she was light years ahead of Josy when it came to brains. Even so, whether I'm being bossed around openly or underhandedly, I still resent it."

"I've always suspected those things about Josy," I said, "but I was like everyone else. I simply couldn't believe that such an apparently nice person could be so self-centered and self-interested."

"Well, watch out for people like that, my darling. A little bit of charm can do wonders when they're trying to get other people to eat out of the palm of their hands. Their supposed niceness puts us off guard, and makes it that much easier for them to get what they want from us."

There was another aspect to all of this that didn't come up in our conversation that day. I was quite sure that my mother must have known that Josy was carrying on with my father, but we never discussed this rather delicate subject with each other. I knew about it, though, because I had come across them in a darkened corridor one day, but they were too preoccupied at that moment to realize that they had been seen. Ever since then, however, I had the distinct impression that Josy was walking around with her nose in the air, very proud to be enjoying a secret affair with my father. She was playing Hagar to my mother's Sarah in the Old Testament narrative, and my heart went out to Sarah.

Josy felt she was on an equal footing with my mom now that she had captured the full attention of the master of the house. She quickly became quite brazen in her efforts to get her own way, knowing that she could appeal to the titular head of the household if my mother objected too strenuously to her underhanded power ploys. She was determined to shinny up the totem pole and nobody, but *nobody,* was going to get in her way.

But she hadn't counted on the hidden strength that lay coiled inside my mother's soul, ready to strike when she was backed against the wall. My mother, who had always hated confrontations and was willing to go to any length to achieve peace through negotiation, was finally at the end of her rope. She had tasted the blessed tranquility that had enveloped her after the death of my grandmother, and she wasn't about to let Josy march right in and put an end to it. She had spent her entire life accommodating her overbearing mother and her self-centered, willful brother, not to mention her egotistic yet charmingly appealing husband. Now it was *her* turn to enjoy some freedom, and nobody was going to stop her this time— least of all Josy.

As she sat on her bed that afternoon, she began to think carefully about her situation. First of all, she resented having been made a victim by the people who were closest to her, and who should have loved her enough to respect her as an individual with hopes and dreams and goals that deserved as much consideration as their own. She had been penalized for her good nature and her conscientiousness in trying to make them happy, but she had to admit that she had gone too far in putting herself and her own needs on the back burner all her life. She had become a doormat, and she blamed herself for having allowed this to happen.

What is it about human nature, she wondered, that seems to make people take advantage of good-natured individuals rather than delighting in them and returning good for good? She had once seen a family of chickens in Juneau turn on a smaller, less aggressive member of their group and pluck all its feathers out, leaving it to die in the cold. What on earth motivated them to do such a cruel, unnecessary thing? Was it all about Darwinism? Was there a mysterious, atavistic urge in those chickens that made them want to rid the family of a member who was thought to be unacceptable because he was less aggressive than the others? Had human beings not been able to get any further than chickens?

My mother didn't have an aggressive bone in her body, but she was observant and practical, and she was nobody's fool. She was certainly able to make decisions that went counter to her basic nature when she was driven to it. It was just that she was so gentle and unselfish that it took her half a lifetime to get to the point where she was finally able to do what tougher people would have done long before, and with far less personal trauma. My poor mom shuddered when she realized what she was going to have to do.

The time had come for her to dismiss Josy.

She thought long and hard that afternoon as she wrestled with the best way to go about this difficult task. She couldn't bear the thought of plucking her feathers and leaving her to die in the cold, although she had to admit that Josy was not at all the kind of person who would just lie down and die. Nevertheless, my mother thought she should at least make the transition a little bit easier by finding her a job. She had lived long enough to know that landing a job was all about connections, and much less about qualifications. The people she knew in Greenwich would probably have been happy to have an energetic, hard-working woman like Josy doing their housework, but could she really recommend her with a clear conscience? Would their husbands be safe?

She finally concluded that she should seek work for Josy in a company or institution that was structured and well-regulated, so her position within it would be unambiguous and not quite so subject to her usual manipulations. Perhaps rules and regulations and the possibility of pink slips would help to keep her in line, although of course there was never any guarantee that Josy, with her vast experience, wouldn't find a way to take advantage of the human factor. Still, my mother couldn't be expected to be responsible for Josy's shenanigans forever.

But who could my mother turn to for help in finding her a job commensurate with her experience that didn't involve working for another family? It suddenly occurred to her that perhaps Emilio could come up with some ideas. It delighted her to think about how they would get together and discuss a knotty problem that would draw them a little closer in the process. She hoped he'd feel pleased that she had thought to turn to him for help and advice.

"So you see, Emilio, that's the whole story," said my mother, who was sitting in the passenger seat of the car in the shade of the elm tree as the groceries waited patiently in the trunk. "Or at least, it's *most* of the story. I don't like to go into the details, if you know what I mean."

"I understand," Emilio said, smiling at her.

He was, in fact, very pleased that she had thought to turn to him for help. He saw it as a sign of trust and respect, and perhaps something more as well.

"It's not possible to be happy when there is difficulty in the family," he went on. "Your house should be a place of refuge, a place where you can find refreshment in the love of your children and many other good things of this kind."

My mother wondered briefly what he meant by "other good things of this kind," but finally decided that he hadn't meant anything in particular.

As it turned out, Emilio invested a great deal of time and energy in finding just the right job for Josy so that Mom would have something to offer when it was time to dismiss her. Emilio came up with a good number of suggestions that they discussed at considerable length under the elm tree, but nothing seemed to be just the right sort of position for Josy's talents and experience.

Then one day they got the break they were looking for.

"One of my buddies over at the pub," Emilio said that morning, "his name is Cookie. He's a big, burly fellow, and he's the best buddy I've ever had. Everybody loves Cookie. Well, he has a wife called Sam, and she said her best friend is a nurse at Greenwich Hospital. So Sam told her friend all about Josy, and the friend said they're looking for somebody just like her to help with geriatric care. They can train her on the job for that."

"Oh, Emilio, *thank* you!" my mother said gratefully. "It sounds like a perfect match for Josy. She was actually very good with my mother, you know. For some reason they both managed to be in control without annoying each other. They had a sort of understanding, I always thought."

"I talked to Sam about Josy when she came to pick up Cookie," Emilio said, happy to have been of help. "She said that domineering people do very well with geriatric patients, who have outgrown the desire to be in control of anybody."

Josy reacted as expected to the news of her dismissal. She did everything she could think of to make my mother feel as guilty as possible about her decision, and when that didn't work she tried threats, anger, sarcasm, vilification, and the silent treatment, but my mother bravely held her ground. Josy eventually attempted to be particularly charming, using blatant praise and flattery in an effort to soften my mother, but all to no avail.

As a final measure she decided to test her influence with my father, but to her great surprise this got her nowhere at all. She had so little understanding of the actual meaning of their relationship that she had not foreseen that he would be delighted to learn that she would soon be leaving the house, thus relieving him of the unpleasant task of having to get rid of her himself, for as far as he was concerned the end of their affair was long overdue.

Things are never quite as simple as they seem. Josy's departure was clearly necessary for my mother's peace of mind, and perhaps an important step in rebuilding family harmony, but it was not altogether easy or uncomplicated to say goodbye to someone who had shared our lives and served us well for so many years. This is partly why it took my mother so long to make her decision, but the alternative would have been completely unfair to her. Even Josy herself, I believed, knew it was time to move on.

CHAPTER SEVENTEEN

Now that I have children of my own, I know that their little personalities are set from the moment they're born. There's no doubt that circumstances have an effect on the way they turn out—the debate about nurture and nature is not one that can or should be resolved. But life with my brothers and sisters in Greenwich was probably very similar to what it would have been in London as far as the interrelationship of the various personalities was concerned. Nurture in this case seemed to take a back seat to nature.

Craig was still the intellectual scientist, always reading "difficult" textbooks and happily explaining them to anyone who had the desire and the patience to listen to his excellent summaries of the material. But he turned eighteen the year after we arrived in Greenwich, so he went off to M.I.T. and we saw very little of him after that.

I was the oldest of the younger group, so it often fell to me to look after little Heather. She was only four when we moved to the United States, so she still required supervision and companionship. She was too young to have interests of her own, and she had no friends to play with since she hadn't yet started school, so she naturally came to depend on the three of us to keep her company and include her in all of our activities.

In time we began to see two problems with this: she was five years younger than Nigel, seven years younger than Wilda, and eight years younger than I was, so her presence was not always understood or welcomed by our friends, who didn't see why she should always be hanging around.

The second problem was that she took it for granted that she was to be included in our activities on a more or less permanent basis, even after she began to go to school. Wilda and Nigel wouldn't even hear of such an absurd proposition, and they made no bones about refusing to let her tag along with them anymore. They had lives of their own by then, and they weren't about to let Heather butt in, so the job ended up in my lap. I figured it wasn't Heather's fault that she was the youngest, and I knew it was very painful to feel lonely and ignored and left out, so I did everything I could to keep her entertained. This was encouraged by my mother, who saw it as a godsend.

"Isn't it lovely to see those two spending time together?" my mother said to Emilio one day when they saw us wading in the lily pond outside the cabaña. "Sonia is like a little mother to Heather."

I was pleased by these types of compliments, as anyone probably would be, but at the same time I felt a bit trapped by a duty that was starting to grow somewhat cumbersome. I had to admit that it was nice to be wanted and needed by my little sister, but I also found myself looking forward to going to college.

The time came soon enough, much to my great relief. I had my heart set on going to Bennington College, a liberal arts school nestled in the hills of Vermont. It was a college dedicated entirely to the pursuit of knowledge for its own sake, and not for the sake of a Phi Beta Kappa key or a four point average.

Applicants had to write essays about why a liberal arts education was important to them, and what they hoped to derive from their education at Bennington. We were also asked to explain how we would be motivated to excel in a system where there were no exams and no grades. This was an easy task for me. I had no trouble writing an essay about reaching for the stars—I was my father's daughter, after all.

The next step was a personal interview with Rebecca Stickney, the Head of Admissions at Bennington College. In an effort to establish what I felt passionate about, she invited me to talk to her about the books I had enjoyed the most in the past year.

Having just graduated from the Greenwich Academy, a college prep school that emphasized academic excellence in the traditional way, I launched into a discussion of some classical literature that I thought would impress her. *The Divine Comedy* leapt to mind, along with *Faust* and works by Corneille and Chaucer and Pérez Galdós. I tried to keep it as international as possible, so that she would know I had a broad reach when it came to literature. I was surprised to see her eyes glaze over.

"What was the last book you read?" she asked, trying to stifle a yawn.

The last book I had read was *Peyton Place.* It was all about incest, abortion, adultery, lust and murder. How could I admit such a thing to the Head of Admissions? I sat there feeling dumbfounded, not knowing what to do.

"What's the matter?" Miss Stickney inquired. "Are you about to sneeze?"

I had to smile at her question. I must have been holding my breath and looking rather red in the face.

"No," I said finally. "It's just that… Well, the last book I read was *Peyton Place.*"

"No kidding!" Miss Stickney cried, leaning forward and looking at me with interest. "That's the last book *I* read, too! Listen, it's nothing to feel ashamed of. It's all about human nature. We can't just talk about one aspect of human nature and pretend the other doesn't exist. What about the Bible, for instance? It's full of stories about all those topics. Well, maybe not abortion, but everything else and more. We can't appreciate what's noble and good if we don't know anything about our baser instincts. We don't always learn by example, you know. Sometimes we learn by antithesis, too."

I knew right then and there that I had applied to the right school. I just hoped they would accept me.

They did, and I flourished in that superb little college. My mother bought me an old car that Emilio's buddy Cookie had recommended (a Buick with buck teeth sticking out over the front fender) so I could drive home on the weekends. I used to look forward to those visits, for the household had settled into a relatively calm and quiet haven now that Josy's disruptive presence was no longer hanging over everyone and creating general havoc.

I say "relatively," because of course our personalities hadn't changed, and the basic dynamics between the siblings were still at work. Even so, we all felt much more relaxed and peaceful, even though I still found myself in the role of "Heather's little mother," especially now that Josy was no longer around. But at least Heather couldn't clamor to go with me on my dates anymore, since they all took place at college.

In spite of these small inconveniences, I looked forward to the weekends. My relationship with Nigel, who was now fifteen years old and six feet tall, was blossoming again. We would escape together in my buck-toothed Buick whenever Heather wasn't looking. I felt guilty about this, but Nigel would soothe my aching conscience by reminding me that she was forcing us into this "fight or flight" predicament by constantly interrupting our conversations, which she found supremely boring, and loudly insisting that we change the subject over to her ten-year-old interests. This would have been okay for short periods of time, but Heather seemed to be a glutton for having it all her way all the time.

She was still too young to have any sense of proportion when it came to sharing time and attention or respecting other people's wishes. My mother had observed what was happening and tried to encourage her to develop friendships of her own, but Heather preferred to seek our company rather than that of her peers. We never could figure out why.

But it all led to a turning point in my life. If Heather hadn't been such a nuisance I probably never would have gone all the way into New York City to find a summer job after my freshman year at Bennington, and if I hadn't found a job in New York that summer, I wouldn't have met the man who would become my husband. His name was Gordon Jones, and he would buy me cream cheese and date bread sandwiches at the Chock Full o' Nuts down the street from our building, where I had found a job as a graphic artist in the same company where he worked.

It was no use trying to have a conversation in the loud and busy Chock Full o' Nuts, so we'd take our sandwiches across the street and eat them in the park. We talked about many things, but Gordon was especially interested in hearing about the innovative approach that Bennington had adopted for our benefit.

"I think it's great that you don't have grades or exams at your college," he said one day. "But how do they assess your progress?"

"We all get assigned to a counselor at the beginning of each semester. They're not real counselors, like the ones who have a degree in psychology. They're just professors, but they keep track of what we're doing in all our courses, and they meet with us once a week."

"So what do you talk about?" Gordon asked.

"Oh, just about anything. Sometimes we talk about the connections between things. You know, like classes that take you on a journey through history and economics and politics and literature and back to history again, looking for ways that one subject affects the others, and vice versa. You can learn so much when you look at things this way."

"I love it!" Gordon smiled. "I wish I could go to those classes with you, but I've already finished college now, so I have to go to work every day. I wish I had appreciated my professors more when I had the opportunity. But my college wasn't quite as exciting as yours is, I'm afraid."

"Don't worry. I'll tell you all about my classes, and we can discuss them as much as you like."

Most people would have shuddered at the thought, but not Gordon. He had an insatiable appetite for knowledge, and was curious about everything. He was the first man I had ever known who was happy to read the same books that I was reading just so we could discuss them in detail when we were finished. We had conversations that would make our spirits soar, and I always looked forward to seeing him.

He kept a 30-foot sailboat at City Island Yacht Club (with books on all the varnished teak shelves below), and he would take me out for a sail whenever I was down in New York on the weekend. One day he told me all about how he wanted to sail around the world on his boat, like Joshua Slocum or Sir Francis Chichester. I wished he could take me with him, but I knew it was impossible. I wasn't ready for that yet. I wanted to stay in school until I eventually got my doctorate.

Gordon had a way of describing the adventure of sailing around the world that made my heart beat the same way it did when my dad urged me to drink deeply from the golden-rimmed goblet of my youth. Gordon was clearly the kind of man who loved life and had undoubtedly taken several long drinks from the goblet of his own youth, so I knew we would have that in common if we decided to cast our lot together.

He wasn't in a hurry, though. I had the impression that he didn't want me to miss any of my classes, and I was glad he felt that way. It was the late fifties, after all, and there were still plenty of men back then who thought that a college education would be wasted on a woman who would then get married and take care of children and grandchildren for the rest of her life.

But Gordon wasn't the kind to just sit back and dream about sailing around the world. He was a man of action, and he was busily training at the U.S. Power Squadron to prepare for his wild adventure. In those days affordable electronic navigational equipment was not readily available to private individuals planning to make off-shore trips in relatively small boats. The Coast Guard wasn't interested in spending its time and money mounting search-and-rescue efforts for poorly-prepared would-be sailors who found themselves in trouble. So yachtsmen intending to make lengthy off-shore journeys had to prove themselves to be competent in taking sightings with a sextant to establish their whereabouts when at sea, and this is why Gordon was taking a class at the U. S. Power Squadron.

Talk about unusual connections! If Gordon hadn't taken that course on celestial navigation we might never have appreciated the true extent of my sister Sheila's special gift. Gordon had come to Greenwich for a weekend visit and he had brought along a stack of books to study for his exam. He sat down on the living room couch after lunch and got right to work. After about forty-five minutes he got up and stretched.

"These questions are killing me," he groaned.

My sister Sheila looked up from her tatting.

"What's the problem?"

"You can't really help me. It's too complicated."

"Too complicated?" Sheila said, not knowing quite what he meant. "Complicated as compared to what?"

We didn't yet know that nothing was too complicated for Sheila. Gordon decided it was easier just to tell her about the problem, and not argue about how complicated it was.

"Well, they're asking where Venus would be if I were in Buenos Aires on February 13, 1938, at ten o'clock at night."

Sheila thought for a moment.

"It would have to be in the constellation Aquarius."

Gordon stared at her. "You're joking, right?"

"How can that be a joke? It's not funny."

Sheila had a totally literal view of the world, and was particularly hard-pressed to see the humor in things. We kids used to love to imitate her saying "that's not funny."

"Well," Gordon said, "it's just that you can't possibly know the right answer without looking it up in the almanac."

"Why can't I?"

Her question was genuine, and she wanted Gordon to explain it to her.

"Well, because the almanac is very long, and contains a lot of information, sort of like a telephone book," he said patiently. "If I asked you what my phone number was, you wouldn't be able to tell me without looking it up."

"Yes, but that's only because I haven't memorized the telephone book."

"My point exactly."

"What?"

"Nobody memorizes the whole telephone book, or the almanac either for that matter. There'd be no point. When we need this kind of information we just look it up, that's all. So you can't know the answer to my question right off the top of your head. You'd have to look up the information in the almanac just like anyone else if you wanted to answer my question about where Venus would be if you were in Buenos Aires on February 13, 1938, at ten o'clock at night."

"Hey, that's pretty good, Gordon," I remarked. "You said that without even looking down at the question again."

"No wonder. I've been struggling with it all afternoon."

"Oh well," said Sheila. "Now you know the answer."

"Right," Gordon sighed, and continued to struggle with the problem while Sheila went back to her tatting.

Around dinner time Gordon looked up from his work and stared straight at Sheila.

"You were right, Sheila! You were absolutely right!"

"I know," she said simply, without a trace of guile.

That was when we found out that Sheila had memorized the entire almanac.

My mother knew that Sheila was unusual ever since she was just a little girl. For one thing, she tended to echo what people said, rather than using language as a direct means of communication. As I mentioned before, she loved repetitive tasks and became frustrated if she was interrupted. Over the years she developed a personal daily routine, and woe betide anyone who attempted to change it or interfere with what she wanted to do. She was particularly talented at performing tasks that required excellent hand-eye coordination. She won many prizes for her exceptionally intricate weaving, and she once crocheted a fifteen-foot altar cloth that was the pride of the local Catholic community.

I knew Sheila had a phenomenal memory, but I never realized it was of truly encyclopedic proportions until the day she told Gordon about Aquarius. When I asked her why she had bothered to memorize the entire almanac, her answer was simple.

"Stars and planets are always where they belong," she said. "That's why I like to think about them."

I had always known that Sheila wanted her life to be orderly and predictable, which is why she spent so much time studying the stars and creating complex designs for her loom, but I had never understood the actual breadth and depth of her knowledge of the laws that govern the universe. She had little interest in the chaotic ebb and flow of human affairs, and was always unsuccessful in her attempts to fit into the workaday world, so she ended up living at home with my mother, where she was at liberty to enjoy her daily routine.

My mother ran the household, as Sheila found it hard to concentrate on things that were clearly peripheral to her own agenda. Although I suspected that Mom might have felt trapped by the responsibility of Sheila's long-term care, she never complained. Once all the rest of her children had left home she was probably glad for some conversation, even if it focused primarily on astronomy and fabric design.

As time went by, my mother's Alzheimer's got worse. As I mentioned earlier, it began with her short-term memory and then moved backward over time as she relived the major events in her life. So she found herself grieving the death of my father, then celebrating the birth of her six children, then joyfully preparing for her wedding day. Eventually she only remembered her childhood in Alaska with Granny and the rest of the Pond family. That's when I learned just about everything I know about Primrose, for she'd talk about him often, thinking she was back in their old house in Juneau, waiting for him to come home for dinner.

By that time Gordon and I were raising a family in Nova Scotia, and we visited her from Canada whenever we could. My mother was a gracious hostess even though she didn't recognize the two rather audacious strangers who behaved as though they were members of the family. We were prepared to arrange for professional care if the situation warranted it, but to our delight and relief Sheila rose to the occasion and started to learn how to take charge. It was a question of necessity now, rather than choice. If she wanted to eat, she'd have to learn to go to the store and do the cooking.

Thanks to her remarkable memory she never needed to make a shopping list or remind herself to pay the bills. What's more, her unusual personality was perfectly suited to dealing patiently with my mother's repetitive questions. It turned out that Sheila had a special talent for caring for an aging mother with Alzheimer's.

She deserved a gold star. No grades, no exams, just a star. But of course, she already had them all, and she knew their exact position in the heavens.

CHAPTER EIGHTEEN

My father died without ever meeting Gordon. I made sure he never did, as he had always seemed to take deep satisfaction in driving away my boyfriends in the past. He would toss them into the air and then fell them with the accuracy of a skeet shooter.

"Tell me, young man," he would say to any boyfriend who dared to come to our house to take me to the Pickwick Theater or to Neilsen's Ice Cream Parlor. "What exactly are your dreams and your passions in life? What do you intend to do to justify your existence as you lard your way over the lean earth?"

The boy would just look at him with a blank expression, not recognizing the reference to Shakespeare. I would try to prepare them for my father's quotes, but he would change them with every new boy. None of them would ever know what to make of him, and they would always remain mute in the face of his baffling questions.

"What was that?" my dad would say, cupping his ear in response to their silence. "I didn't quite catch that."

"Come on, let's go," they would urge me, helping me on with my coat. "It was nice meeting you, sir," they would say over their shoulders as they hustled me out the door.

Then I would never see them again.

Looking back on it today, I was sorry that Gordon had never met my father. He would have had the maturity to handle it a little better than the other boys, but it would have been a grueling experience for him even so. I had the feeling that he would have passed muster, though, but now it was too late. He would never know the scary yet compelling man that was Kay Harrison—the man who could never sit still, the man with enough energy to lead an army, the man who had the spirit to dream impossible dreams and hold a room full of people in thrall with his engaging observations about the human comedy.

He died of a heart attack just as my grandmother had, but not because he was elderly. His heart attack had been brought on by the stress of his overly active and challenging life, combined with a diet consisting mainly of butter and Béarnaise sauce. His doctors warned him that his lifestyle was not conducive to good health and a long life, but he invariably answered them with a diatribe about the merits of a short and exciting life versus a long, dull one. The doctors would shake their heads and do what they could to ease the pain of his latest outbreak of gout. They knew better than to try to argue with their headstrong, non-compliant patient.

My father reacted to his heart attack just the same way as my grandmother had responded to hers. He thought he was having severe indigestion, so he simply took some Alka Seltzer. When that failed to relieve the pain, he took some Aspirin and lay down for a nap, fully expecting to wake up feeling refreshed and ready to meet the challenges awaiting him that evening.

Oddly enough the Aspirin was probably not such a bad idea in that it thinned his blood and gave him a little extra time, but those precious moments were wasted while he did his best to tough his way through what he assumed was just a severe episode of heartburn. He thought that because he had suffered so many bouts of indigestion, his esophagus must have become chronically inflamed. The digestive juices from reflux had probably eaten their way deep into the lining, and the pain had increased accordingly.

So much for self-diagnosis.

He was at the Beverly Hills Hotel that afternoon, and was preparing to make a special presentation to a group of film producers that night at dinner. When he didn't show up at the appointed time, one of them decided to call his room.

After failing to locate him either there or at his office, the producers eventually dispersed, assuming that my dad would eventually get in touch with them to reschedule the meeting. Three hours later the housekeeper went to his room to turn down the bed and discovered him lying on the bedspread, showing no signs of life. She sounded the alarm and he was immediately taken by ambulance to the hospital, where he was pronounced dead on arrival. It was an abrupt and rather commonplace ending to an extraordinary life that had been lived with brave determination and unceasing passion.

I was awakened at three a.m. on December 7, 1962, by a doctor who informed me of my father's death. He had tried to contact my mother, he said, but had been told that she was in the hospital. Was it a serious matter, or could he call her there? I told him he could go ahead, as she was scheduled only for a minor operation that morning. He had apparently already contacted Craig and Nigel, but had been unable to locate Wilda, who didn't answer her phone. He knew that Sheila and Heather lived at home, so he said he would ask one of them to keep calling Wilda. Meanwhile he'd phone the hospital immediately to try to intercept the surgeons before Mom was wheeled into the operating room.

My mother was duly rescued from the surgeons, and Emilio arranged for a flight for her to go to Beverly Hills for Dad's funeral. Craig and I flew down from the Bay Area, where we were both graduate students at the time, and Nigel flew in from Tucson, where he was attending the University of Arizona. We all felt shocked and distraught, but we were glad to have the chance to talk with one another and compare notes. Mom told us that Heather didn't want to come, and that Wilda still wasn't answering her phone, and Sheila was better off staying home. So it was just the four of us.

The next morning we went to a viewing in the funeral parlor in Beverly Hills. The four of us approached Dad's open casket and gazed at him as he lay there engulfed in folds of white silk, wearing a dark suit and conservative tie.

He had the same uncanny "presence" about him, even in death. My first impression was one of total astonishment to see him lying there, looking as though he were still alive and just taking a peaceful nap. I had never seen his face reflect such serenity. On the rare occasions when I had seen him napping in the past, I noticed that his powerful jaw muscles would be working, as though he were chewing over some challenging problem even as he slept. But now his strong, craggy face was no longer intimidating. It reflected instead the sort of quiet, mature wisdom he had always sought and never found when he was living in the grip of his ardently passionate nature.

The funeral itself was scheduled to take place the next morning. A few things stand out in my memory as I look back on that day. After we all got into the black limousine that was waiting to take us to the service, the well-meaning doorman waved goodbye and told us to have a nice day.

It was a perfectly natural thing for him to say. He hadn't noticed that we were all dressed in black, and he really had no way of knowing that we were on our way to our father's funeral. But his words rang in my ears like a message from a mocking deity who wanted to remind us that life had no meaning at all, and that the one time in our whole lives that we would be saying goodbye to Dad forever would be just like any other normal day for us and for everyone else. It would be a "nice" day.

I looked over at Craig and Nigel and my mother, but they seemed not to have heard the doorman's parting words. They were just sitting there lost in their own thoughts as the limo pushed forward into the traffic.

It was a small funeral, considering the importance of my dad's significant contribution to the growth and development of the film industry, but I do remember that Roy Disney and Walter Winchell signed the guest book at the funeral parlor. I felt deeply touched that these two busy men had taken the time to pay their respects, and from that day onward I've always tried to go out of my way to attend funerals and sign guest books. People always keep those guest books, and the signatures provide comfort for years to come.

My mother behaved with great dignity and composure throughout the proceedings, as though she were living in a parallel universe where nothing was actually what it seemed. She acted as if she were outside herself, calmly observing some other family as the members attended a funeral.

But when we got back to our suite at the Beverly Hills Hotel, she suddenly let go of all her pent-up emotions and began to cry with loud, agonizing sobs of despair. I stood there motionless, unable to stir, powerless to provide relief or encouragement. What was wrong with me? I had always been the comforter and helper, but there I was, frozen in place, useless, paralyzed, in a state of shock as I witnessed her grief.

It was at that moment that Craig came alive. He sat next to Mom and put his arm around her, reassuring her that Dad was now in a better place and at peace with himself and the world. He told her all the usual things, but his words were like magic, like a healing balm, and my mother lingered on his every word, nodding and smiling at him through hot tears of hope and desolation. He was her handsome boy, and she looked at him tenderly, as though she were thinking how lucky she was to have this son, this gift left behind by Kay to provide her with comfort after his final curtain.

The moment, as such moments often are, was suddenly interrupted by the loud, intrusive ring of the telephone on the writing desk. Nigel jumped up and answered it.

"It's for you, Mom," he said. "It's a man called Paul."

"Paul?" my mother echoed, her face lighting up. "It must be Paul Preston! I don't know any other Pauls."

She got up and eagerly took the receiver from Nigel. I can't write down what Paul had to say, since I couldn't hear his side of the conversation, but my mother's answers remain with me to this day.

"Hello?

"Yes, this is Marion Belle…

"Why Paul, this is such a surprise…

"Oh, thank you. I appreciate that…

"Yes, he was a great man. He had a unique personality…

"What was that? You read about it in the papers…

"I see. So you spoke to Sheila…

"Ah yes, of course. She gave you this telephone number. That was very resourceful of you, Paul…

"What? She knew it by heart? Well, I'm not surprised…

"Yes, of course…

"I know. My mother is gone, Edwin is gone, Bart Thane and Big Fay and Laura have left us, and now…

"No, Paul. You mustn't think of it that way. Little Fay is still with us. And you still have me. I care very much…

"You have all those people at the hospital who love you and need you. You've done wonders for them…

"I can't go up to San Francisco this time, dear Paul. I have to get back home. I can't leave Sheila…

"Yes, I promise…

"Yes, I will. I think of you, too…

"I love you, too…

"Don't worry, Paul. I know how you mean it…

"I know you better than anyone else. I would never misunderstand you…

"I will. Thank you so much. I'll always remember…

"Goodbye, Paul. It was so good to hear your voice…

"Yes, always. Goodbye, my dear friend."

My mother hung up the receiver and sat down on the couch again, looking pensive. She had spoken to Paul in short, loud, staccato sentences, as though the telephone were still a brand-new invention.

After a few moments she began to talk about Paul and how they had grown up in Juneau together. His father was a mining engineer who had worked for Bart Thane. Paul was the brightest boy in his class at school, but he was also the humblest and the most generous-hearted, helping the teacher by tutoring the slower students with their lessons. Edwin had liked him from the moment they met, and they became very close chums, even though he was two years ahead of him in school. My grandmother greatly approved of him because he set a good example for Edwin with his excellent manners, his brilliant scholarship, and his gratifying respect for his elders. My grandmother often said he could do anything he wanted with his life. He was a boy who would go far, she was quite certain of that. He had a great future ahead of him.

Apparently Mr. Preston finished his mining projects at just about the same time that Edwin developed heart trouble, so my grandmother traveled back down to San Francisco on the same boat with the Prestons. Later Paul became Edwin's tutor since he had to stay home, so Paul went to the house every afternoon to teach Edwin everything he had learned at his own school that day.

"So *that* was his name!" I exclaimed. "Paul! You told me all about Edwin's tutor and how you once had a crush on him, but you never told me his name."

"What? I told you I had a crush on him? I don't recall saying that," my mother said, blushing slightly.

"Mom, it's nothing to be ashamed of! I'm sure you had very good reasons. He sounds perfect."

"He *was* perfect, as a matter of fact. But he was Edwin's tutor. My mother wouldn't have liked it if we had gotten involved. It wouldn't have been easy for him to concentrate on his tutoring program."

"Why didn't you marry him later, then?"

"You're much too curious, So."

"Well, why didn't you?"

"He never asked me, that's why."

"Do you think he wanted to?"

"I'll never know that, dear, since he didn't ask."

"Mom, don't try to duck out of it that way. What did your heart tell you?"

"I knew he was fond of me. I could sense it, and that kept me interested in him."

"Well, then?"

"Your father isn't even buried yet, and you're asking me how I felt about another man."

"You're right, Mom. I'm sorry. You're right."

We all sat there in silence, thinking about Dad.

"Don't worry, So. I'm thinking about him too," Mom continued, as though reading my thoughts. "Paul, I mean. His voice brought everything back to me. It's funny how that happens when you hear somebody's voice for the first time after so many years. It was just as though he were standing right here in this room. It was as if no time had passed since I last saw him."

I didn't dare say anything, but Mom apparently felt it was okay to keep talking about Paul after all.

"Little Fay kept in close contact with him," my mother went on. "She lived near San Francisco, in Niles, so she saw him every time she went into the city. She was married but there was nothing between them, no hint of anything, so they felt free to see each other as often as they pleased. With us it was a bit different. Once I got married it wasn't easy to keep up the friendship, so we didn't see each other anymore. But Fay told me his news. I was grateful to her for that. We were all such great chums."

"So what happened, Mom? Can you tell me?"

She gave a deep sigh and looked thoughtful for a while, then she made up her mind to go on.

"Well, I've told you already how he came home from the war with shell shock, and how he ended up in the mental hospital. Afterwards I found out from Fay that he became so depressed that he fell into a catatonic state and never said a word to anyone for many years... I don't know how many. The poor man! Such a terrible waste of a wonderful brain and a beautiful heart. And he was such a good-looking man, too. Everybody said he looked like Rudolph Valentino.

"But then something extraordinary happened. Paul had been thoughtfully observing the other patients in his ward, even though he never spoke. He began to realize that in general they were suffering terribly because they had a lot to say but they didn't know how to express it, and nobody had time to listen. So they just sat around feeling depressed, and eventually they gave up trying to communicate with anyone. They'd rock back and forth, and mutter to themselves, and the doctors would just increase the level of their medications.

"So then one day Paul saw one of them trying to get an orderly to listen to him, but he was too busy and wouldn't stop to pay attention. So the man just sat down and cried. He cried bitterly, like a heartbroken little boy, and Paul just couldn't stand to see him like that. He got up and spoke to him. They talked and talked till it got dark, and when it was time to go back to their rooms for the night, that man was a different person. Or maybe he wasn't different. More likely he had returned to some version of what he had been before. But however you look at it, Paul had given him back his life. He managed to heal that young man because he understood him better than a healthy person ever could, and he had the gift of a great teacher. He was able to explain things clearly and simply, and he could always find the right examples and the best analogies, so he made sense to the people he talked to. He got through to them when nobody else could."

She stopped and thought about Paul for a while.

"That's such a beautiful story, Mom. I can see why you loved him."

"I did. I thought the world of him, and I still do."

"So then what happened? What became of Paul?"

"They hired him at the mental hospital to help the other patients. It was such important work, and Paul did it so well. He used to talk about it with Fay. It worked the other way, too. When the patients got better they gave Paul the feeling that he was making a difference, and it gave him the strength to go on."

"Well, so did Paul get better too, then?" Nigel asked.

"In some ways he got much better, but the hospital became his whole world. He lived there, you know, so it protected him too much from real life. He began to live in his head a lot more than was good for him. It's never too wise to have that much time to ponder. It's much better to work and mingle with ordinary folks, people who are living normal lives, whatever that means. But you know what I'm saying."

"I could go visit him, Mom," I said.

"That would be lovely, dear. I know he'd like that. It's always nice to make a special effort for someone who has dedicated his whole life to helping others."

"Would you like me to order room service, Mom?" said Craig, looking at his watch. "It's dinner time already."

"I think that would be very nice," my mother said. "I don't feel like dressing up for dinner. I feel exhausted. And thank you, So dear, for helping to take my mind off Kay for a little while. You've all been wonderful."

I was always astonished at how incisive my mother's remarks were when it came to understanding other people's feelings. I had been sitting there feeling guilty for spending so long on the subject of Paul, rather than reminiscing about Dad and trying to be a comfort to Mom in her time of grief. But perhaps we had all needed a change of subject for a little while. There would be plenty of time for grief. It would come back in waves and waves later on.

But sometimes it would be positive grief, the kind that touches you and inspires you and makes you recall things that are uplifting about people who are gone. Things like the way my dad treated Paul on his wedding day. My mom said to me years later that Paul told Little Fay that it was one of the most inspiring moments of his life. It had been his turning point. It was the day he realized that there was still hope in the world, and that happiness existed after all. My father the atheist had put Paul back on the road to faith.

CHAPTER NINETEEN

After my father died, it seemed strange to me that the world didn't come to an end. But it was business as usual. People just kept right on with their normal routines as if nothing had happened, which made everything seem rather surreal to me. Even *we* had to go back to what we had been doing before Dad died. Nigel returned to the University of Arizona to work on his BA, Craig went back to Stanford to write his PhD dissertation, I resumed my MA program at UCB, and Mom went back to Greenwich to take care of Sheila. Life went on. We were all having a "nice" day, but nothing would ever be the same.

I'd never get any more letters urging me to drink deeply from the gold-rimmed cup of my youth, or to throw myself with wild abandon into the arms of life, or to reach for the stars with all the strength and determination I could muster. Now it would be Dad's turn to drink deeply from the cup whose mysteries only he could understand, and if a new life called to him from another dimension somewhere, he would undoubtedly throw himself into it with unbridled enthusiasm. At least I hoped that this would be the case, but I had been hanging around academia long enough to know the rampant cynicism that is inevitably expressed regarding the sort of truth that eludes the scientific method.

Did science have to trump spiritual matters every single time? Why was the scientific method so highly regarded and so quickly accepted even in the humanities, where a creative imagination should be encouraged? My mother was thinking about the same thing at the same time.

December 15th, 1962

Dearest little Señora,

    I want to thank you for all your kindness and support, and the concern you showed for me after Daddy died. I'm sorry you had to see me in such a state, especially when you were suffering so much yourself. I don't like to dwell on all this, or bring up this nightmare again, but I felt the need to tell you how deeply comforting it was for me to have you and Ni and Craig with me at the funeral.

    I know what you mean when you say you feel as though you're living in some sort of dream and just going through the motions. It is indeed a very strange feeling to look at the people walking down the street, going about their business as though nothing had happened. You're right, the whole world should stop! Daddy was your world, and mine too, so I can understand what a strange feeling it is for you to observe that your world and the outside world don't seem to coincide at any point.

    Life will never be quite the same without him. Even though he was hardly ever here, we both knew there was a presence somewhere thinking about us sometimes, and you must never forget that he loved you very much, even though he didn't know how to say so. Many men are often like that. They tend to be closed-mouthed about their inner feelings, which they consider to be pure sentimentalism. They seem to be embarrassed to talk about such things.

    Maybe someday, in another life and in another world, things will be different. It's impossible for me to believe this is all there is. I don't know how it's all going to work out, but it would be senseless for us to be born and die in a world that is largely a vale of tears with little comfort other than love, which all too often seems sporadic and unsatisfactory for many reasons, the chief one being that we're all just fallible human beings. No, there has to be more, or life is meaningless.

Daddy always pounced enthusiastically on the idea of meaninglessness, though. He felt it was heroic to embrace life with a spirit of bravado, in spite of everything. But how could he feel so very passionate about what was essentially random and meaningless? It's hard for me to get excited about an empty hole.

Maybe I'm no better than Big Fay Thane and Marion Todd, those dyed-in-the-wool wishful thinkers. I suppose grief is making me overly philosophical, or else maybe it's releasing philosophical thoughts that I didn't know I had. All I know is that God is there, but I don't know what he's thinking any more than an ant knows what I'm thinking.

But someday we'll see him face to face, as "the Spiddit" used to say. That's what Edwin called our minister in Juneau. He had an English accent and he was always talking about the "Holy Spiddit" in a very solemn voice, and we kids used to scream with laughter about it on the way home.

I think of Juneau often these days. I miss Primrose so much, and I wish I could be with him now. I can even smell his pipe as I think about him. It's funny how sometimes we can feel like children, even when we're old!

I'm rambling and I'm sorry, my little pet. I think maybe we all go slightly insane when crises happen. But I promise you I won't talk this way anymore. What you need right now is a strong mother to comfort you. I'm sorry I'm not there with you in California, but how can I be in five places at once, when my children are so spread out?

I must run now, my dearest. I have so many things to do. I want to put some decorations up. Christmas will be special this year. A time of hope and promise.

Eternal love from your maman

Eternal love. Could those words have been prophetic? Is there indeed a place where love can be eternal? My mom mentioned that she felt wistful and philosophical because of her grief over Dad's death, and I was feeling the same way. So much so, in fact, that I asked my professor and mentor, José F. Montesinos, whether he believed in God. He smiled and was about to say something humorous and dismissive, but then he hesitated a minute, remembering my recent loss and my probable state of mind. He looked at me thoughtfully for a moment, then he told me he didn't believe in absolutes, adding that nobody could possibly be expected to know, with even the minutest certainty, if God existed or not. He patted me on the shoulder and advised me not to trouble myself too much about things that could never be ascertained one way or the other.

There are lots of things, indeed, that we can't know and even more things that we can't prove, but I wasn't ready to give up on knowing with the heart as well as with the mind. What about the love my mother spoke of, that provides our only comfort even though our human frailties sometimes make it sporadic and unsatisfactory? I would *hate* to live without love just because it can't be seen with a microscope. The same thing goes for hope, trust, faith, and yearning— and even passion, scary and dangerous as it might be. The rest is meaningless, just as Mom said.

When I wrote to her and told her about how Monte felt about absolutes, she had this to say:

I was sorry to hear that Mr. Montesinos threw cold water on your question about God. Intellectuals have a tendency to be ultra cynical about things that are difficult to prove in a rational way. They seem to trust the head much more than the heart, but this only closes the doors to a large segment of reality that can only be perceived and appreciated by the heart and the spirit.

Don't be discouraged by his reaction, my darling. Just enjoy his intellectual qualities, and refrain from discussing spiritual matters with him, as those types of conversations will probably go nowhere and end up being very frustrating to you. Remember that he and his intellectual friends fought against Franco, who was closely associated with the Roman Catholic Church, so any mention of religion would make his hair curl, as he probably associates religion with right wing politics. I think religion and politics make poor bedfellows, and should stay well away from each other. So just keep on cultivating your brain, but listen to your heart in all matters concerning God and his mysterious, inscrutable purposes. You can safely believe in him, no matter what anyone says. But keep your opinions to yourself, otherwise you will find yourself embroiled in endless and useless arguments that could leave you feeling very discouraged about the whole subject.

Emilio Romero was a godsend for my mother after Dad died. Now that Josy was gone, they were free to spend as much time as they wanted chatting in the car under the elm tree, or anywhere else for that matter. They spent hours talking with each other in the house, in the gardens, and especially in the cabaña that was in a courtyard filled with flowers, statuary, and symmetrical hedges. Emilio loved this small one-room dwelling, for it reminded him of the resting houses on his property in the pampas of Argentina. He would always look forward to relaxing in these cabañas after a long day's work with the cattle, and he particularly looked forward to the sirloin steak with *chimichurri* sauce prepared for him by the women who took care of these properties.

My mother, who was a wonderful cook, wanted to round out the nostalgic effect that the cabaña had on Emilio by filling it with the delicious odor of chimichurri sauce to greet him after a hard day's work on her own property. She found a recipe involving olive oil, paprika, rosemary, thyme, and garlic. This could have been a marinade from almost any country, but what made it typically Argentinean was the addition of a chopped chipotle chili in adobo sauce.

When Emilio smelled the sizzling steak and chimichurri sauce emanating from the cabaña, he was seized with such a strong and pleasant sense of nostalgia that he held my mom in his arms and danced cheek-to-cheek with her around the table. This was the beginning of a new stage in their love, but my mom would never tell me anything more. It was something that belonged to them and to nobody else, and I rejoiced for both of them. It was the one time in her life when she could enjoy complete freedom, without having to keep her private matters a secret from Granny or Josy, and without needing to be concerned about the consequences of entertaining my father's knight in shining armor.

My mother did tell me, though, that the first year of her romance with Emilio Romero was one of the most joyful years of her life. Even though she was in her late fifties, which to a young person might be considered relatively "old," that year seemed to last forever. She used to describe it as her year of living dangerously. Dangerously close to complete bliss, dangerously close to heaven, dangerously close to the sun. She was always afraid that she would wake up and find that it was just a dream, or that like Icarus, she had fallen back down to earth on wings of molten wax. But if it *was* real and not just a dream, she was afraid there would be a price to pay, like the price of an addiction to heroin. Would her heart try to stabilize itself and plunge into the depths of despair before it could find an equilibrium some-where in the middle? Was this happiness just a prelude to misery and sorrow? They say that passion burns itself out as quickly as a brush fire. Would the time come when there was nothing left but the taste of ashes?

My mother was no coward, however. Although she had to admit that these questions occasionally occurred to her, she nevertheless threw herself into the arms of her happiness with as much abandon as my father always did. All I know is that she drank deeply from the cup of her love for Emilio, and Emilio joyfully shared his cup with her too, the same way he had shared his lemonade with her when they had first been struck by the *coup de foudre.*

My mother and Emilio shared many glorious years of deep, faithful, enduring, compassionate love, the kind my father had always sought and never found. I suspect that he was influenced to some extent by the opinions of his peers in England who looked down on my mother for being from a hopelessly uncultured, uncivilized place somewhere in the frozen north. Her gentle, unselfish nature and charitable attitude were not qualities that my father considered very "interesting," yet they turned out to be the underpinnings of a love that united my mother with Emilio and gave them a quiet, lasting happiness that neither of them had ever felt before, and that far exceeded their expectations. They both marveled at how they had had to wait a whole lifetime to enjoy true love in their old age.

Then, toward the end, the Alzheimer's disease picked up its pace. The early forgetfulness that had bothered me when she always arrived late to get us from school was doubtless caused by a mind troubled by worries, but now it was more a question of a brain invaded by plaque.

Emilio took it all in stride. When she forgot little things, he made lists for her. When she couldn't recall where she had left her glasses or her hot water bottle, he would find them for her. When she was confused about where she was, he gently guided her home again, and when she told him stories about Juneau, San Francisco, Tokyo, London, and Greenwich, he listened with careful attention and genuine interest. He wanted to know everything about her, right down to the last detail, and her condition inspired her to talk about all her memories with the clarity of a person who had just lived them that very day.

"I have to fire Josy," she told him one morning. "I've been fretting about it all night. I feel sick about it. I *hate* having to fire people. She's been with us such a long time, you know."

Emilio thought it was best to tell her the truth. Perhaps if he reminded her that she had already been through that painful experience, she would remember it and move on.

"Josy has already left your employment," he told her. "She is in Greenwich Hospital. Do you remember now?"

"What!" my mother exclaimed. "She's in the hospital?"

"No, no. She is *working* in the hospital. She has a job there. She is very happy with her new work."

"Wasn't she happy here with us?"

Emilio thought about that for a while. If he encouraged my mother to believe that Josy had left of her own accord because she had found a better job, maybe she wouldn't be fretting so much now and feeling so guilty about firing her. It saddened Emilio that she had to feel guilty about it at all, especially now that he knew about Josy's dalliance with her late husband.

"She was very happy," Emilio told her. "You gave her a good life with your family. You rescued her from the Nazis, and you provided her with every comfort. You gave her everything you could. But there was one thing you could not give her, and that was her independence. People need to be independent in order to have self-respect. So you have given her a very great gift. You have given her the freedom to be independent, and I know she is grateful to you for that."

My mother had listened to him attentively, and seemed to be satisfied with his answer. She was relieved and happy for about an hour, and then she began to worry again about how she was going to approach Josy with the news that she was fired.

Emilio was learning more about my mom than he would have if she had not been suffering from Alzheimer's disease, for she was unable to hide what was on her mind from day to day. She spoke to him quite openly about all the things that troubled her and made her feel guilty. He listened thought-

fully to what she had to say, then he found ways to absolve
her of her guilt by assuring her that the people she believed
she had wronged were actually the ones who, in many cases,
had done her the most harm. Besides, he was quite sure that
they themselves had never been wronged by her. Why, he
wondered, was she so willing to blame herself rather than
placing the blame where it really belonged?

On another occasion Emilio came across my mother in my
grandmother's room, looking at the books on her shelf.

"*Here* you are, my love!" Emilio exclaimed. "I've been
looking all over for you."

"My mother was so well read," said my mom, looking at
him pensively. "She knew all these classics like the back of
her hand. She could have derived great wisdom from them,
and she probably did, but she was never able to apply any of
the principles to herself. She was very perceptive when it
came to judging others, but she knew almost nothing about
herself. Don't you think that's strange?"

"Yes, I do," Emilio admitted. "Why do you think she
was like that? To what do you attribute this?"

"We're all a bit blind when it comes to seeing ourselves
as we really are. But over the course of a lifetime we begin
to catch glimpses of ourselves in the mirror that other people
hold up to our faces. We have to be very brave to take a good
look. Maybe my mother didn't have that kind of courage.
She started out with a lot of courage, but she used it all up
having to face her sorrows and hardships."

"I always thought that courage increases when it is used
frequently to face difficult situations," Emilio remarked.

"I suppose that's true sometimes, but it depends on the
person. Maybe it's more a question of honesty than courage,
this business of looking at oneself in the mirror. But we all
have to do it sooner or later. That's when we find out how
desperately we all need to be forgiven for our mistakes."

Mom closed the book she had been looking at and put it back on the shelf in Granny's room. Then she turned toward Emilio, sighing deeply and looking thoughtful.

"My mother died last night," she told him. "It was right after we had a lovely Japanese dinner. We took her to the hospital, but it was already too late."

"She was very old," Emilio reminded her. "She had a good life. You took excellent care of her. You gave her a room of her own, and a beautiful house to live in."

"You're right, Emilio. Yet she often used to complain that she was just like a bird in a gilded cage. She was never satisfied with her life. She was always complaining about everything. There's so much about her that I don't understand, even to this day."

"She must have made herself unhappy. It is not healthy to have such a pessimistic view, especially when people are doing their best to take care of your needs."

"There was something strange going on at that hospital last night," she continued, as though she hadn't heard what Emilio had said. "There was a geisha girl standing there the whole time."

"A *geisha* girl?" Emilio repeated, looking surprised. "In the hospital room?"

"Yes. She was the same one I used to see when Kay and I were living in Japan. She would stand by our bed at night, looking at us while we slept. I didn't feel very comfortable about that."

"I should think not!"

"She didn't scare me, though. She had kind eyes and a gentle, knowing smile. I had the strong impression that she was very wise, but that she was sad about something even so. I never could figure out just what it was she wanted, or why she took such a great interest in us."

"Maybe she knew what lay ahead."

My mother looked at Emilio and smiled.

"Maybe so. It's funny, though. I never saw her again after we left Japan. Until last night at the hospital, I mean. I wonder what she was doing there."

Occasionally my mom would hurt Emilio without meaning to. One day when he was happily singing his favorite tango music, she gave him one of her "stop that" looks, which is the way she would look at us when we were doing something she didn't approve of.

"What is wrong, *mi amor?*" he asked, going over to her and stroking her hair.

"Well, I really don't see why you need to ask me such a question," she replied, frowning at him.

"Darling, what is it?" Emilio said, enfolding her in his arms. "Tell me why you are so sad today. Please tell me."

My mother burst into tears.

"Don't you know that Kay died today?" she sobbed. "You shouldn't be singing tangos at a time like this."

"*Ay, mi vida, mi vida,*" Emilio murmured, with tears in his own eyes. "I cannot bear that you are suffering this day all over again."

"All over again? What do you mean? We haven't even been to the funeral yet. I'm not quite sure where it is. I was hoping you'd take me in the car."

"Of course I will take you in the car. Meanwhile I'll wait in the living room while you get dressed."

"Thank you so much. I'll just slip into something more appropriate. I'll be out right away."

After waiting in the living room for over an hour, Emilio finally knocked gently on her bedroom door. He listened for a moment or two. When there was no answer, he peeked inside to see if she was all right.

She had fallen asleep on the bed. Emilio took an extra blanket from the closet and gently covered her with it. Then he kissed her lightly on the forehead and tiptoed out of the room.

The next morning she woke up in tears. Sheila had come in with her breakfast, and didn't know what to do.

"What's the matter, Mummy?" she asked her, using the British name she had learned as a little child. It was the first name she had ever used for Mom, so it was the "correct" one as far as she was concerned.

My mother sat up in bed and stared at her.

"Why, how can you ask such a thing? Your father died this morning!"

"No he didn't," Sheila corrected her in a matter-of-fact tone of voice. "He died on December 6th, 1962."

"All right, he died yesterday, then. Why do you have to split hairs?"

"No, it wasn't yesterday," Sheila insisted. "It was, let's see, it was fifteen years ago next month."

"You're talking in riddles," my mother replied, looking a bit irritated. "He didn't die fifteen years ago. You shouldn't make up things like that. And I don't know what you mean by saying he died next month. You're not making any sense at all."

Sheila stood there frowning and twisting her lip, not knowing what to do.

"I'll call Emilio," she said finally, putting the breakfast tray on my mother's bedside table.

"Is there some gardening for him to do?"

"No, there isn't. It's too late in the year for gardening. It's the month of November now."

"Well then, why call Emilio? Isn't he the gardener?"

CHAPTER TWENTY

After my mother's funeral we six brothers and sisters all went with our spouses to Manero's steakhouse on Steamboat Road to talk about Mom and to reminisce about the old days. Manero's was familiar to all of us, for we always used to go there to celebrate birthdays and any other occasion that came up. We would order Gorgonzola salad, chicken Parmesan or rib eye steak with fries, buttery garlic bread, and an ice cream roll for dessert. Mom would have just loved to be there with her "bairns," as she used to call us, but we could never convince her that all that rich food and red meat constituted a healthy diet.

Heather, who was the last one to leave home, had quite a bit of information about my mother's final years, but it was Sheila, of course, who was the repository of all knowledge, both past and present.

"Mummy often used to come to Manero's after the rest of you left home," Sheila remarked, as we took our places around the table.

"She did?" said Nigel, looking surprised. "It's funny that she came here so much after we were gone. I love this place myself, but Mom was used to eating gourmet food, after all those years of hanging out with Dad."

"Yeah, what's with the steak and fries all of a sudden?" Wilda wanted to know.

"Mummy liked Manero's because it was where Emilio wanted to eat," Sheila explained. "He liked red meat because it reminded him of home. He was from San Luis, Argentina, where his family had 8,000 hectares of land. They raised beef cattle on it. The original homestead was constructed by the Jesuits, and it served as a staging post for the patriots on their way to Chile, where they enlisted in the Liberation Army of General José de San Martín. I heard Emilio telling Mummy that one day."

"*Thank you,* Sheila," Wilda said.

"You're welcome," Sheila smiled.

"Does anyone have anything less *historical* to say about this Emilio guy?" Nigel asked. "Who was he, anyway?"

"I've never heard of him," Craig said. "Nobody ever tells me anything."

"Well, you should visit more often," Wilda suggested.

"He's the gardener," Sheila told us.

"Is that all?" Nigel said, perking up. "Just the gardener?"

"None of your business," Sheila snapped.

"Whoa!" said Nigel gleefully. "Have I stumbled on a juicy piece of gossip?"

"Emilio was Mummy's *friend,*" Sheila said.

Sheila was right, as usual, for where there is true love, there is always deep friendship as well.

"What's the scoop, Heather?" Nigel persisted.

"It's true. They were an item."

"Cool!" Nigel exclaimed. "I'm glad for her."

"What do you mean?" Sheila asked. "What kind of an item? An item of what?"

"Mom hired him to take care of the house and grounds," Wilda said. "He did a terrific job, too. He kept the place looking spick-and-span, so now we should get a good price for it when we put it on the market."

"What?" Sheila said. "You can't sell Mummy's house! She wouldn't like that."

"Well, we can't really afford to keep you there either," Wilda said. "It's a little big for just one person. But don't worry. We'll find a nice place for you. A small apartment near Greenwich Avenue, so you can walk to Gristede's when you need groceries. We'll put you close to the Catholic

Church, too, because when Emilio leaves, you won't have any way to get around, you know. You'll have to hoof it."

"Hoof it?"

"You'll have to walk."

Sheila sat there looking worried.

While the guys were settling the bill, I turned to Sheila and told her that Gordon and I would give her a lift home. I wanted to see our old house one last time before it got sold, and I was hoping to be able to meet Emilio and thank him and say goodbye before we set off on our long journey back to Nova Scotia.

"Thank you, Sonia, that would be very nice," Sheila said politely, ever mindful of my mother's instructions on the use of good manners.

As we drove up to our house in Belle Haven I saw two tall, white-haired men talking on the brick veranda at the front entrance. They were so deep in conversation that they didn't even hear Gordon as he came to a stop on the driveway and pulled up the emergency brake.

I recognized one of them as Paul Preston, the elderly gentleman who had spoken that morning at my mother's funeral about his love for his angel, Marion Belle. I also remembered how she had talked to him on the telephone on the day of my father's funeral. Then, as the other elderly man came into focus, I recognized him as the one who had joined Paul and the pastor at the front door of the chapel just before my mother's funeral service was over. This other man, I realized, must have been Emilio Romero, but his back was toward me. I checked with Sheila just to be sure.

"Yes, that's Emilio standing there, but I'm not sure who he's talking to. I think he might be Paul Preston, because when he spoke at the funeral he called Mummy by her real name, Marion Belle. So he's probably the same childhood friend from Juneau that she used to talk about sometimes. At the funeral he spoke about the First World War, and about how he got shell shock, and he said he was Uncle Edwin's friend, so therefore he must be Paul Preston."

"That's right. It took me a whole hour to remember his name, but it came back to me at Manero's."

As I approached the two men, I realized that Paul had never seen me before, although he might have heard about me from Little Fay, and Mom had probably told him stories about all her children.

"Ah, Sonia!" Emilio exclaimed, taking my hand in both of his. "It's so good to see you. Now tell me, have you met your mother's friend, Paul Preston?"

Paul was too shy to give me his hand, but he did smile and stare for a while before he looked back down at his feet. It was gracious of Emilio to make the introductions. He must have had to think quickly to figure out that Paul and I had probably never met. By this time Sheila and Gordon had joined us, and I introduced Gordon to Paul.

"Won't you come in?" I said, as I walked toward the front door. "Paul, I've been away for a while, so I'm not sure where everything is and how to be a good hostess, but Sheila will help me. And Emilio, maybe you'll entertain the men in the living room while we look for something in the kitchen."

"Please, you don't have to put yourself out for us," said Emilio. His sentiments were echoed by Gordon and Paul, but Sheila and I paid no attention.

"Mom would have wanted me to serve refreshments," I said, after I had settled them in the living room.

The fridge had nothing in it but a carton of milk, a bottle of cranberry juice, some tofu, half a red pepper, some alfalfa sprouts, a few eggs, and a jar of capers.

"Sheila, you must be half *starving*!"

"I don't feel hungry, so I can't be starving."

When I looked in the cupboard I found nothing but some Raisin Bran and a box of Saltines.

Sheila and I made some little canapés with the crackers and the rest of the ingredients that were lurking in the fridge.

Then we poured the cranberry juice into wine glasses and put everything on a tray.

"What are you going to do for groceries now?" I asked Sheila. "Would you like us to stock your fridge?"

"Emilio will take me to Gristede's. He always takes me on Thursday mornings. That's tomorrow."

"Will milk and Raisin Bran be enough for breakfast?"

"That's what I always have."

"How are you fixed for money?"

"I go to the bank before I go to the grocery store."

"Where does the money come from?"

"Daddy. He left me an annuity."

"Thank God."

After we had our cranberry juice and canapés, Sheila took Gordon to show him her weaving, leaving Paul and Emilio and me to reminisce about Mom. I expressed some sorrow about the relationship she'd had with my father, thinking that it must have been disappointing to her in many ways. But Emilio assured me that she'd found her marriage to be even better than expected, in that Dad had lived up to her belief that life would never be boring with him.

As for Paul, he had provided the faithful friendship that my father couldn't give her. They had never seen each other again after she had married Dad, but they'd stayed in touch over the years. They had shared their hopes, joys, fears, and insights, and they'd held on to each other through all the ups and downs of their lives.

And then along came Emilio, who provided her with the romance that my father had only been able to lavish on other women. Emilio had loved her with the passion that she had dreamed of and yearned for, and she returned it with all her heart. It had struck them as amusing and amazing that they had both had to wait until their final years before they had been swept away by the perilous, powerful fire of romance. But because they were old, they appreciated every minute of their time together and they were grateful for the blessing of the notorious *coup de foudre,* which has always had such a bad reputation as far as staying power is concerned. Passion should only be doled out to the old, they decided, for only the old have the wisdom to sustain it.

I understood that afternoon that thanks to the three men in her life, my mother had had it all: excitement, faithful friendship, and romance. I was happy for my mom, and the discovery that her three men had made her life fulfilling was a great comfort to me.

But what about her children? Had we given her the joy of maternal love? I had some serious doubts about my own contribution to her happiness as a mom. I had nursed a guilty conscience all my life for having confronted her one day with all those unfair and bitter accusations when I was a teenager. I had always meant to apologize to her one day, but I had put it off over and over again, fearing the powerful emotions that could have come spilling out, and not knowing where they might have led. Now it was too late. I touched on the subject as we sat there talking, but I didn't elaborate on the cause of my guilt and sorrow.

"You can tell us about it," said Paul. "Maybe Emilio and I can be of some help. Maybe your mom already talked to us about what's troubling you."

My first reaction was to think to myself that they would hate me if they knew how cruel I had been that day. They had both loved my mother, and they would be saddened to hear how I had treated her. I didn't blame them, either.

"I can't tell you," I said, tears welling up. "I don't want you to know how much I made her suffer. It would only make you suffer, too. And plus, I don't want you to know what a horrible person I was."

Emilio got up and came over and sat beside me.

"I think I know what it was, and maybe I can help," he said. "If I'm wrong, it doesn't matter. But I think you ought to know that your mother suffered deeply with the regret of sending you to California when the war broke out. It was a decision she had to make quickly, on the spur of the moment. People were all looking for ways to keep their children safe, and the lucky ones were able to send their children far, far away to Canada and to the United States, where the Germans would never get them. It was considered a privilege to have the means and the wherewithal to send them so far away. The further away, the better. Is that what it's about?"

"Yes," I whispered, but I couldn't say any more.

"Your mother told me about that day when you were a teenager. You thought she sent you away because she didn't love you. You told her that if she had loved you she would have come with you, and she wouldn't have made you live with your grandmother and Miss Ava. You said that if she had really cared about the safety of her children she wouldn't have had three *more* children during the war. It was all a mystery to you, and you felt terribly angry and also guilty about your anger."

"She told you all this?" I said, embarrassed to the core. I felt like a mortified teenager all over again, who had just been caught doing something unthinkable.

Paul hiked himself off the couch with the help of his cane, and sat right opposite me on the coffee table. Luckily it was a good, sturdy piece of furniture.

"You're a casualty of the war, just like me," he said. "War has a peculiar way of making us feel guilty for things we can't help. Shell shock has a lot to do with feeling guilty. I felt guilty that I was alive when most of my buddies were dead. I almost couldn't bear it. I wanted to die, too."

"It's true you had nothing to feel guilty about, Paul," I said, "but I did. It wasn't fair of me to tell my mom that she sent me away because she didn't love me. It was the exact opposite of the truth. I made her suffer unnecessarily. She didn't deserve that."

"You need to know that she also felt very guilty that she sent you away and didn't come with you. But she was young then, and she couldn't bear the idea of leaving your father

alone with his mistresses. She wanted to stay and fight.
Have you ever heard of *Sophie's Choice?*"

"Yes. I've seen the movie."

"Well, the Nazis did the cruelest imaginable thing when
they made Sophie choose between her two children. She
chose to save the boy, and the Nazis put the girl to death.
But imagine how that girl would have felt about her mother
if she hadn't really died... if she'd been able to talk to her
later about her choice after the war."

"It would have been terrible. Unthinkable."

"Yes, it would have. So don't you see? Your feelings
about your mother's choice are so understandable that your
mother herself was never able to forgive herself for choosing
your dad instead of going with you."

"Really? Did she tell you that?"

"She wrote me about it in her letters. Yes."

"Poor Mom," I said, through my tears.

"That's what she said about you, too. She wrote to me
about you all the time. She loved you with all her heart."

"And now she's gone. It's too late for me to say how
sorry I am!"

Paul leaned a little closer.

"That's where you're wrong. She knew how sorry you
were. You didn't have to say anything. She understood."

"Thanks for telling me that, Paul. You're an angel."

"No, your mother is the angel. I meant what I said this
morning at the funeral. My speech was pretty terrible, I
realize that. I'm not much good at public speaking. But I
meant every word I said. Your mother was an angel, and she
saved my life."

"And you just saved mine."

"If I did, it's because she sent me. Did you feel her with
us this morning? Did you feel her there?"

"Yes. I did."

"Well, she was smiling. Did you feel that, too?"

"Yes."

"Give me a little smile, then. It would make her happy."

Paul stood up, and Emilio too, and we all had a group hug. I felt enveloped in the love that these men had shared with my mom for so many years. We would miss her as much as any heart can miss another human soul.

"I have something I'd like to show you," Emilio said. "I think you'll like it. Come with me. Shall we get Gordon and Sheila?"

He led us all out the kitchen door and down the back stairs. We followed him dutifully in the direction of the cabaña. I was pleased to see the excellent job he had done with the grounds. The grass was cut, the hedges were neatly trimmed, and the hydrangeas were in bloom. But I wasn't prepared for what I saw next.

When Emilio opened the gate to the courtyard where the cabaña was, I couldn't help sucking in my breath in awe and amazement. The high brick walls were covered with pink, white, and purple morning glories intertwined with coral-colored honeysuckle. The flowers were alive with butterflies feeding off the sweet nectar in the trumpets, and songbirds twittered in the bushes and vines. Emilio had laid down a beautiful flagstone path through the middle of the courtyard, leading to the cabaña.

"This was our own personal garden," he said. "We spent many hours together in this spot. I always thought we could both live out our lives here, but I understand that you have to sell the big house, and it's impossible to separate the cabaña and the courtyard from the rest of the property. But we loved it here for as long as it lasted. In the last years, of course, your mother didn't know where she was or who I was, so it's not really quite so bad to have to move away."

"Even so, Emilio," I said, "this is a beautiful testament to your love for my mom. I can't get over it. Most men would give their women a single rose as a token of their love, but look what you've done. You've given her a whole botanical garden!"

"Well, it's nothing compared to the big house that the original owner shipped in from Andalusia, brick by brick, for the woman he loved. I've just added a little full stop, as the British would say."

"My mom was lucky to be loved so much by three such remarkable men; my dad and the two of you."

"There was one more man in her life as well," Emilio said. "She talked about him all the time in the last year of her life."

My heart turned over. What? There was *another* man? What new secret was about to be revealed?

"Yes," Paul said. "I knew him well. He was a brave, upstanding man. I would often think about him whenever I felt like just giving up. There were times in my life when I wanted to lie down and die. But he was my inspiration. He gave me the strength to go on."

My mind raced around, trying to think who Paul and Emilio were referring to. I couldn't remember my mom ever mentioning anything about another man. He must have been someone she had known in San Francisco, because she was only ten years old when she had left Alaska, so she was too young for romance back then. Who could he have been? I looked at Paul and then at Emilio, searching for clues. But they only smiled and waited. They seemed to be sure that I knew about this man.

Then I remembered my mother's Alzheimer's disease, and how it had taken her backward through time. So who would the last man have been?

"Percy Pond!" I exclaimed. "The first was the last! What's *wrong* with me? How could I have forgotten my grandfather? My head is so full of romantic notions that I completely forgot about one of the strongest kinds of love there is, the love of a father for his child."

"That's why God calls himself our father," said Sheila, right out of the blue. She had been standing there all along, but she was so quiet that we had forgotten she was there.

"That's right, Sheila," Paul said, putting his arm around her shoulder. He felt her stiffen slightly, and he quickly took his arm away. He took no offense, however. He seemed to understand instinctively that she didn't like to be touched, and he respected her boundaries. But he also knew that she understood a great deal about love, even though she had no idea how to express those feelings, and no particular desire to do so, either.

"You often refer to Percy Pond as Primrose," Gordon said to me. "How did he ever get that nickname, anyway?"

"It was my Uncle Edwin's nickname for him, but I don't really know why he called him that. Do you know, Paul? You were a great friend of Edwin's. Maybe you can tell us where the name Primrose came from."

"I can indeed," Paul said. "I was right there on the day when the name took root, so to speak. Your mother and your grandmother and Edwin and I were all huddled around the kitchen stove at their house in Juneau, waiting for Percy to bring home the bacon, as your grandmother used to put it. We were all quite hungry, and Hattie had sent him to the butcher to buy some pork chops. We were talking about the pork chops and how good they were going to smell and taste when they came out of the sizzling frying pan. Just then Percy came in waving a bouquet of flowers and a package wrapped in brown butcher paper. Hattie just ignored the flowers and ripped open the package, only to find it had seal meat in it.

"Well, when she saw the seal meat she was absolutely furious, and demanded to know where the pork chops were. Percy explained that he didn't have enough money for pork chops *and* primroses as well, at which point Hattie exploded. She told him the primroses were just typical of how absurdly impractical he was. He tried to explain that they symbolized *her*, in that primroses were rare and beautiful and weren't native to Alaska, but she refused to listen to anything he had to say on the subject. She said that all she wanted were *real* pork chops and not symbolic ones, or poetic ones, or photos of them or anything else that wasn't real.

"Your grandfather said his love for her was real, but she wasn't having any of *that*. Then she ran out of the kitchen, leaving Percy to fry up the seal meat. And from that day on, Edwin called him Primrose, and the name caught on. We all thought Primrose symbolized *him* more than it did Hattie, for he was not only a rare man with a beautiful, poetic soul, but his love was real, even if he did bring home seal meat instead of pork chops."

We all stood there together in the garden, thinking about what Paul had said.

"Emilio, what a perfect touch!" I exclaimed suddenly. "Why didn't I notice these before?"

There before us, on either side of the flagstones leading to the cabaña, was a profusion of primroses in purple, white, yellow, and lavender. I looked at Emilio with the deepest admiration.

"My mom must have *loved* those primroses. They lead straight to the place where you shared your hearts and your lives."

"Yes," Emilio said. "It was the place we called home."

"It gives a whole new meaning to the primrose path," Gordon observed.

"Amen," said Paul.

"Hear, hear," I added, raising my glass.

"To the primrose path that leads us home!" Emilio said, clinking my glass.

"I'll drink to that!" Paul chimed in. "The way to heaven doesn't have to be thorny every step of the way. We can always plant primroses, can't we?"

It was good to hear Paul and Emilio laughing together with their arms around each other, like old friends.

"That's not funny," Sheila muttered under her breath.

Epilogue

Sheila Harrison moved to downtown Greenwich, where she continues to do her embroidery and crocheting.

Craig Harrison received his PhD in philosophy from Stanford in 1969, and became a philosophy professor at the University of California in San Francisco. After his first wife, Marion, died of cancer, he married Julie Riley. He is now retired and still living in California.

Sonia Harrison received her PhD in Romance Languages from Harvard, and became a Spanish professor at Dalhousie University in Halifax, Nova Scotia. She married Gordon Jones in 1970, and co-owned and operated a dairy products manufacturing plant with him in Lunenburg, Nova Scotia (Peninsula Farm Ltd). They have both had several books published since their retirement in 2002. They have two daughters, **Valerie** (Doty), a physician and cartoonist, and **Victoria** (Grassmid), a retail manager with M.A.C. Victoria has a son, Harrison, and two daughters, Alexa and Danica (identical twins).

Wilda Harrison received her BFA in fine arts from Rhode Island School of Design. She married Barry Walter and had two children, **Seth** and **Eve**. Later she married John Gallagher, a historian and published author. Now a widow, she works as a webmaster and graphic artist at CUNY (Brooklyn College).

Nigel Harrison attended the University of Arizona, then began working on the PAVE PAWS radars in 1972, while an employee of Control Data Corporation. He wrote the radar interface, communications control, and the graphics display drivers in machine language, and his code runs to this day at the Cape Cod site. The CDC computers at the four other sites have been replaced with modern machines, but use emulators so they can run Nigel's code exactly as it exists (at a savings of just under a billion dollars per site). He is married to Rebecca King, a Presbyterian minister. He has two children, **Emily** and **Juliette**.

Heather Harrison received a BSN from the Greenwich Hospital School of Nursing, and an MSN from Bridgeport University. She married Timothy Grimes and has two children, **Lauren** and **Todd** (a graphic artist and a computer animator for the movie, *Barnyard*). She is now married to Scott Hurley, a fellow nurse.

The property in Belle Haven was sold and the buildings torn down due to damage caused by the freeze/thaw cycle of the winter months. The physical appearance of the seven acres on the corner of Walsh Lane and Otter Rock Drive is no longer recognizable to the Harrison family, but the memories remain.

Appendix

Biography of Lloyd V. Winter and Edwin Percy Pond, Alaska State Library

Lloyd Valentine Winter (1866-1945) and Edwin Percy Pond (1872-1943), of the firm *Winter & Pond*, were prominent Alaskan photographers. In 1893, Winter came to Juneau from San Francisco and opened a studio in partnership with George M. Landerkin, known as Landerkin and Winter. In 1894, his longtime friend E.P. Pond bought out Landerkin. Winter and Pond served as official Alaska photographers for the Alaska-Yukon Pacific Exposition in Seattle in 1909. During the gold rush, Winter was appointed official photographer for the firm, Underwood and Underwood, and the publication, "Leslie's Weekly," to cover gold rush activities on the Dyea and White Pass trails to the Klondike. Winter & Pond operated their Juneau-based curio and photography studio for over 50 years until Pond's death at age 71 in 1943. In 1945, Winter turned the business over to Francis Harrison who maintained the Winter & Pond Co. until 1956.

Lloyd Winter and Percy Pond preserved the legacy of Alaska's past through their photographs, taken over a period of 50 years. The studios of Winter and Pond Company in Juneau, Alaska, provided local residents and visitors with a rich perspective of Alaska that is now considered a unique reflection of the state in the early 20th century. During the company's existence, Alaska expanded mining, fishing, and resource development into profitable ventures that transformed it from a frontier district to a thriving territory of the United States.

The portraits that Winter and Pond produced show the diversity of Alaska's people through the years, from the gold rush of the Klondike in 1898 to the end of the mining operations in the Juneau Gold Belt District during the 1940s. Above all, Winter and Pond made an outstanding contribution to our understanding of Tlingit Indian culture by photographing traditional Tlingit social customs and cultural activities just prior to the rapid changes of the 20th century.

Lloyd V. Winter (1866-1945) and E. Percy Pond (1872-1943) arrived in Juneau in 1893 to find a prosperous mining community that was on the verge of developing the multi-million dollar Juneau Gold Belt. Communities from Thane, Douglas, and Treadwell to Windham Bay, Point Sherman, and a half a dozen load mines were thriving mining locations by the early 1900s. For 50 years, Winter and Pond photographed the growth and decline of the mining industry in Alaska and Canada. The 1,200 mining photographs in the Winter and Pond Collection provide a significant insight into the operations and living conditions of the hard rock mining industry.

As the partners watched Southeast Alaska thrive, they also observed the Tlingit culture cope with the social changes thrust upon it. As adopted members of a Tlingit family, Winter and Pond had an intense interest in the Tlingit culture and the impact of foreign settlement on the lives of Southeast Alaska's natives. The partners recorded traditional activities such as potlatch gatherings and dances. The 350 images of Tlingits are evidence of the photographers' admiration of the rich heritage of the Alaska Native people and reveal an intimate view of Tlingit customs and social conditions.

During their careers as professional photographers and businessmen, Winter and Pond chronicled Alaska's history by recording the boom towns, ships, miners, and landscapes in a unique style of photography that represented Alaska's frontier and growth. They also produced several publications, including *Types of Alaska Natives* and *Totems of Alaska.* Today, viewers recognize the Winter and Pond photographs as a valuable documentary of Alaska's past.

Winter and Pond operated their Juneau-based curio and photography studio for over 50 years. In 1945, two years after the death of Percy Pond, Lloyd Winter turned the business over to Francis Harrison [no relation to the Harrison family described in this volume], who maintained the Winter and Pond Company until it closed in 1956. Thousands of original glass plates and nitrate negatives were stored until 1981, when William Jorgenson, a Juneau resident who knew Winter and Pond, donated the images to the Alaska State Library. Mr. Jorgenson's efforts were instrumental in the preservation of the glass plates that are now viewed by local residents and people from around the world wishing to catch a glimpse into Alaska's past.

Excerpt from a letter written by Heather Harrison (née Marion Belle Pond) in 1955:

Greenwich.
Sept. 4th.

Sonie my dearest,

Here is a little note to greet you at your Charles St. abode, before you take flight to God's country! So I hope you get this before you go!

I loved the letter addressed to the Famille Harrison, and long for a detailed account of your sea-side visit. I'm sure your green eyes have been opened to many delightful aspects of European life in general as well as French life in particular, truly admirable people, the French. How much better you'll be able to understand them spiritually when you're able to speak to them in their own language! You do, so you've probably noticed this. I think you're a girl that will be very proficient in foreign languages, & take keen delight in learning them. I can see ahead of you a whole glowing panorama of interesting life situations, and due to your intelligence, you'll have as few gloomy shadows as possible, in them. Everyone encounters some of these, as they go along, but I firmly believe that the brain and the free will are able to minimize them, and that's where common sense comes in. That's a quality that borders on the divine, but like the house-wife, gets little attention nor much praise, but when something's wrong with its performance, the apple cart is very effectively upset! Another thing is very lucky for you, and that is that you have Leo for a father, so you can peruse his literature and drink in his knowledge and the poetry that's in his mind and soul! Just think - you're Kay Harrison's daughter - what a wondrous advantage that is for a girl! It puts me in mind of a remark that was made by my supervising teacher years ago when she met him and grew starry eyed at the wonder of him - "anyone who has the honor of bearing his children should have as many as she can."

Anyhow, here he is, we've had the warmth and the humour of him ever since he walked briskly out of the airport, settled into the car in business-like fashion as if he'd never been away!

I guess by the gist of my last letter you gathered that the trip to Maine was a great success, and our journey back lots of fun. Heather got her way about the cabins

Excerpt from a letter written by Harriet Hall Pond to the author:

Fri. July 29/55.

My dear Wanderer!

I have just read a good long letter you wrote Mamma – so! they accost you on the rues of Paris do they – you should buy a domino and wear it over those alluring orbs of yours. Your letters are so interesting and you seem to know your Paris very well from the outside. Has anybody asked you how you like the beautiful Rose Window over the Entrance of the Madeleine. That is the standard old joke on Americans who often "enthuse". I wasn't so very wrong as I acknowledged not noticing it. The fact being there is no Rose Window, tho most cathedrals have them. Have you been to the fabulous Notre Dame.

I'm sure Kay has taken you to the DOME where they serve coffee & liqueurs to crowds and if you sit & watch the moving crowd long enough you'll see, so they say,

some body you know. T. Fay & I saw
a very handsome white
Russian we knew in Juneau as a youth
and an ex. engineer - such a dancer
too - But something snapped and that
young chap coasted down hill very fast.
His mother was a handsome aristocrat
she rented my house from me when
I took your baby mother & Edwin to Calf
on a trip in 1907.   This last war
may have done away with that Peri
patetic school of philosophy & sight seeing that was popular before the war.
    I recall when I was studying History
of Greece I was intrigued with their
beautiful culture in such ancient
times (att. 5th Cen. B.C.) and when I
came across Aristotle & his peripatetic
school I immediately started my
rote studies by learning "out loud"
while making my bed or other chores.
My lessons were learned with out effort and my room was always neat
before going to school. Susie had to
make the coffee & toast & my cold lunch.

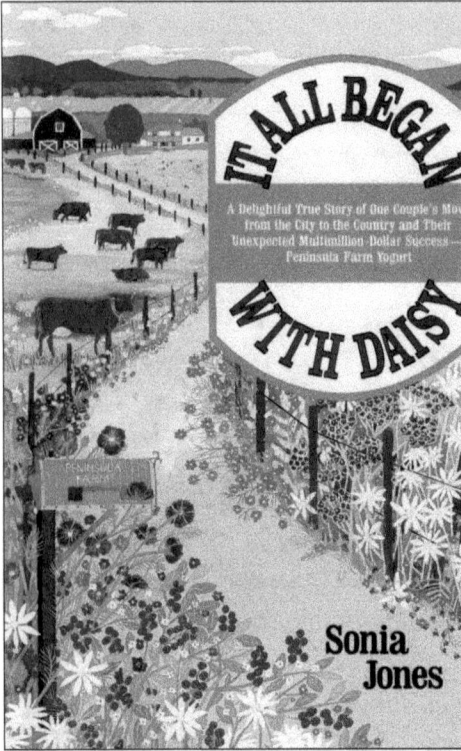

When Sonia Jones moved with her husband to Nova Scotia to teach at Dalhousie University, they bought an oceanside farm and settled down to enjoy a life of quiet contemplation. But they bought a cow in an unguarded moment, and their tranquility evaporated overnight. Daisy quickly became the head of the household, providing them with more milk than they knew what to do with. They started making yogurt for a local health food store, eventually reaching over two million dollars in annual sales. This is their story—hilarious, maddening, and chock full of great information on how they survived when the going got tough. Published by Penguin (Dutton imprint) in New York.

What critics are saying about "It All Began With Daisy"

The eponymous Daisy is a cow the author and her husband bought when they moved from New York City to a farm in Nova Scotia. Daisy's yield of milk proved to be so plentiful that the author was able to make yogurt for local store owners to sell. As the fame of the product spread so did its sales. The author relates the story in an engaging fashion, even describing setbacks cheerfully. There is added charm in accounts of veteran farmers whose advice was invaluable to the couple, to whom rural life at first was utterly alien. (Publisher's Weekly, May 27, 1987)

Some stories have inherent charm... To describe her unusual achievements, the author has constructed a breezy, well-paced narrative, with nice descriptions of the Canadian countryside and cheerful character sketches of her neighbors and business allies. Inverting the conventions of business autobiography, she describes her blunders, both technical and in matters of human relations, with a pleasing comic style. Indeed, the best things in "It All Began With Daisy" are its author's good humor and genuine charity of spirit. (Bob Coleman, New York Times, June 21, 1987)

What's especially interesting about Jones' story is that her company became a success in spite of itself. It was in business before it even had a name, it had no plan and no start-up money. That's nothing short of amazing when you consider that everything written or said on entrepreneurship stresses developing a solid business proposal, having a sound marketing plan and spending a small fortune to launch the enterprise. (Marilyn Linton, Lifestyle Editor, the Toronto Sunday Sun, June 21, 1987)

The inevitable growth of the house that the Joneses built is funny, but there is a more telling side to the story of these entrepreneurs. Starting with sound bees in their bonnets about quality and honesty, they had to deal constantly with the strange logic of bureaucrats and the curious customs of bigger businesses such as supermarket chains. They appear to have hung in there with astonishing and unceasing good humor. (Pauline Carey, Toronto Globe and Mail, August 8, 1987)

****+This is the inspirational book to read when you know the grass is greener on the other side of the subway fence and you want to get out of the rat race... the Joneses are now celebrities thanks to their high-quality products and their funny and heart-warming story. For an old-fashioned, delightful experience, read this true-life romp of two urban professionals let loose on a farm. (Kathryn Falk, Nonfiction Reviews, Aug., 1987)

A colorful parade of well-drawn characters and comic-tragic events from a leaky filling machine to three years of production built upon a kitchen stove and Canadian Tire Styrofoam coolers - all but ensures the Jones' life will soon be the subject of a made-for-TV movie. (Would Jane Fonda consider playing the confident and unstoppable Sonia?) Other cast members include Travis, the laconic neighbor who offers homespun advice on everything from plumbing to bovine psychology; David Sobey, the fairy godfather who "discovers" Peninsula Farm and invites the Joneses into the Sobey supermarket chain; Yvette, a French-Canadian dynamo who regales her health food customers with sensual descriptions of strawberry yogurt; and Ed Shoemaker, the grasping chain store buyer who teaches Sonia the hard, cold facts of the food industry. When it comes to business, muses

Sonia Jones, "small is terrifying but medium is beautiful." The yogurt Queen has arrived. (Jennifer Henderson, the Toronto Financial Post, November 9, 1987)

It All Began With Daisy is a non-fiction romp for those who enjoy good writing, humor, and country life. The joy of this delightful book is that the author keeps the reader amused and interested in the many trials and tribulations experienced by an academic combining a farm and business career, to say nothing of raising a family at the same time. Readers will acquire a favorite new author after reading this book. *Jim Morrison, Burrelle's The Book Corner, Nova Scotia, 1987*

What readers are saying about "It All Began With Daisy" on Amazon:
5.0 out of 5 stars
Customer

"It All Began With Daisy" is an inspiring book filled with humour, local colour and excellent storytelling. It is encouraging to read of the adventures of such an entrepeneurial couple and their "vigourous muddling" through the years of establishing their yoghurt company. Characters come alive and conversations quiver with the skill of the author's recounting. Highly recommended for light, inspirational reading.

5.0 out of 5 stars
L. Watson (Louisiana) - (REAL NAME)

When I first read this engaging book by Sonia Jones in about 2000, I couldn't put this book down. Closing the last page, I attempted to look up the Peninsula Farm, envisioning a trip to Nova Scotia, only to find the farm recently shut down.

Available on Amazon or www.erserandpond.com

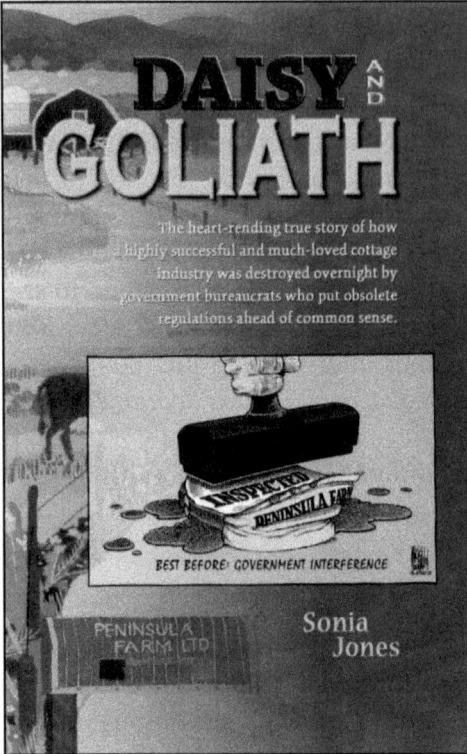

DAISY ᴬᴺᴰ **GOLIATH**

The heart-rending true story of how a highly successful and much-loved cottage industry was destroyed overnight by government bureaucrats who put obsolete regulations ahead of common sense.

BEST BEFORE: GOVERNMENT INTERFERENCE

PENINSULA FARM LTD

Sonia Jones

Competition from a successful small business is not always welcomed by big business interests, so Goliath rose up to challenge Daisy. The poignancy of the betrayal of Citizen Daisy by her own government is palpable.

Yet this book is not just an attack on the co-consipiracy of big government and big business. The story of Daisy and Goliath, like all good parables, crystallizes the issues and provides us with hope for a better future.

This tale is particularly relevant to the questions facing us today concerning interference from big government, and the important contribution of small business to the well-being of the economy.

Available on Amazon or www.erserandpond.com

The

YOGOURT

COOKBOOK

by Sonia Jones

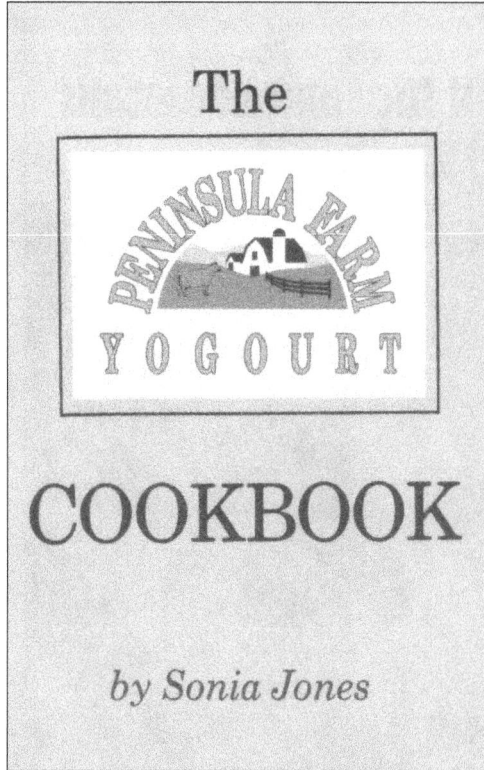

If you have ever wanted to make your own yogurt at home, this is the book for you. Sonia Harrison Jones, a highly successful producer and purveyor of gourmet yogurt for twenty-five years, reveals her tried-and-true recipes along with instructions on how to make delicious yogurt (and what to do when you fail).

This well-loved book is a compendium of yogurt fact, yogurt lore, yogurt recipes and all you need to know to become part of the yogurt revolution. Press the "contact us" button at www.erserandpond.com

Available on Amazon or www.erserandpond.com

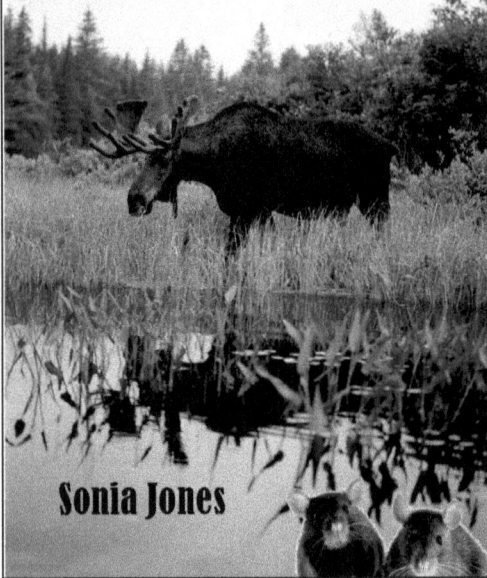

Of Mice and Moosecalls

Reflections on life ever laughing

Sonia Jones

This is a humorous, beguiling collection of topics ranging from warbling church mice to operatic moose calls, and from chaos on the farm to wild roosters running amok in the Dutch countryside. Illustrated with some of the best color images and photography from artists all over the world, this beautifully written collection of personal anecdotes will touch both your heart and your funny bone.

Available in an edition without photos.

Also available on Amazon or www.erserandpond.com

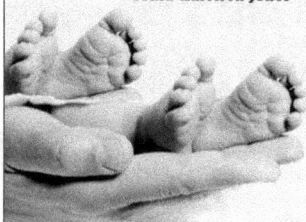

When linguist Lisa Maxwell goes to the Basque Country to seek the unknown origins of the language, she meets some enigmatic characters in a lost village in the Pyrenees. Who is stealing relics from major cathedrals in Spain, and why? What's going on in the secret, secluded biotechnology lab? What role does Rh-neg blood play here? How do genetics and linguistics combine to unlock the mystery of the origin of humankind? Is it possible to clone Jesus? If not, why not? If so, what are the consequences?

What readers are saying:

This is a masterpiece. It was a real gripper. My wife and I almost fought to get to read it. — Rev Clarence Vos, pastor and retired professor, Calvin College, Grand Rapids, MI

I LOVED it! For me the test of a good book is that when I'm not reading it I'm thinking about it and trying to figure out when I'll be able to get back to it. That definitely happened to me with this book. —Julie Graveline, retired Canadian naval officer

Available on Amazon or www.erserandpond.com

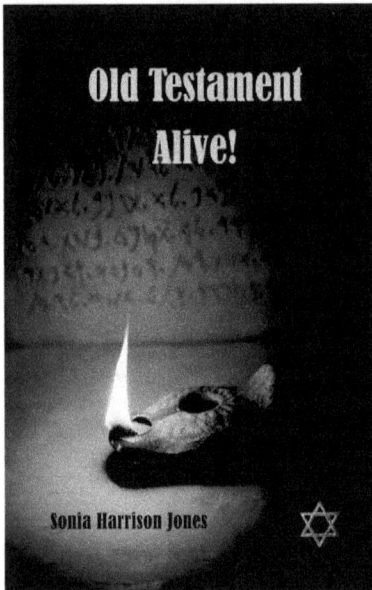

Old Testament Alive!

Sonia Harrison Jones

This is a poignant, respectfully humorous bird's eye view of the Old Testament, when people in the Scriptures come alive and talk directly to the reader. The prophet Hosea wonders why God wants him to marry a prostitute, and Satan boasts about winning people to his point of view. This fascinating book is illustrated with 170 beautiful color images created by professional photographers around the world.

What readers are saying:

As a pastor, I was delighted to discover such an interactive study. When we shared the Bible with our very bright int'l students, we used this book to inform our discoveries and launch us into discussions. —Rev Winston Clark, pastor

We found this book very informative and entertaining. It is one of the reasons why my wife and I became Christians. —Dr. Cheng Wang, pathologist

Available on Amazon or www.erserandpond.com

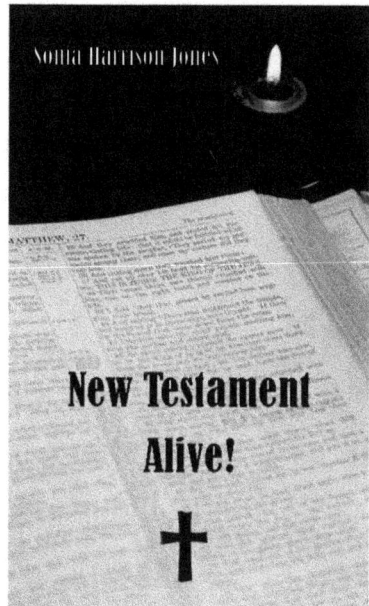

Sonia Harrison Jones

New Testament Alive!

✝

This sequel to *Old Testament Alive!* presents an overview of the main events of the New Testament, where people come alive and talk to the reader. Lucifer returns as a cool and worldly young man who presents an ironic and cynical view of the unfolding action. Judas explains his political ambition, Peter bares his soul to you after he denies Jesus three times, and Paul plays a crucial role in introducing and explaining the new Christian faith.

What readers are saying

When we studied with Dr. Jones, we went back 2,000 years when people in the Bible talked to us about their struggles and hopes and fears. The class reminded us that we are all one human family, no matter when and where we live. It was so joyful and fun to join a group of people to discuss the Christian faith. —Yiling Hu, MD, MSc, and Changjiang Li

Available on Amazon or www.erserandpond.com

The Choir

Sonia Harrison Jones

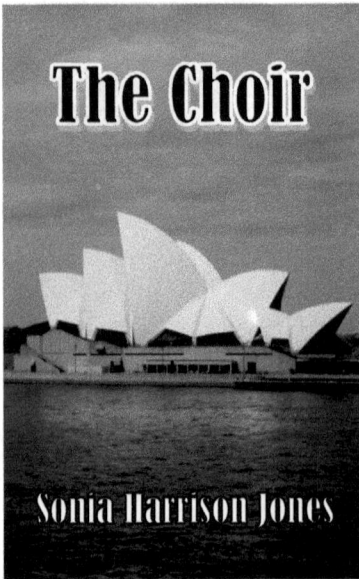

This is an unusual mystery novel where lurking danger combines with inspiring Broadway songs, providing sensitive insights into the human condition. The plot includes two love stories, topped off by the choir's once-in-a-lifetime performance at the Sydney Opera House, leading to a poignant and uplifting finale.

What readers are saying

This is a must read. Dr Jones displays great storytelling ability and crafts a tale of suspense, intrigue and humor bundled with romance, sophistication and existential issues related to self worth and purpose. Dr Michael Lawrence, neuropsychologist, Michigan

I was intrigued by this novel right from the opening chapter. I was led through a gripping story, beginning with unintentional identify theft and then on to the high seas, with rich characters forging deep connections through serendipity and chemistry. I didn't put the book down until I had savoured the epilogue's satisfying revelations. A terrific read! Janet Manuel, poet and choral singer, Nova Scotia

Available on Amazon, Kindle, or at www.erserandpond.com

Other books by Sonia Harrison Jones (see also Sonia Jones) available on Amazon:

Alfonsina Storni: A biography of the famous Argentine writer, published by G.K. Hall, Boston, as part of the series *Twayne World Authors*. Jones won a Canada Council grant to do her research in Buenos Aires. She also published several articles about Alfonsina Storni while she was in Argentina.

What readers are saying

Dianna MacKinnon Henning, Delivered Conference Paper, 20th Century Literature Conference—Univ. of Louisville, 1990:

The spirit that Alfonsina Storni possessed and the difficulties she surmounted can best be relayed by quoting Sonia Jones's "Final Appraisal" in her book entitled Alfonsina Storni: "After a careful reading of the entire corpus of Alfonsina Storni's work—her seven volumes of poetry and miscellaneous poems, her dozens of plays and short stories, and her scores of essays and articles—one is left with the feeling that this prodigious output is perfect testimony to the incredible courage and stubborn determination she had to possess in order to get around the many obstacles that would have prevented lesser women from ever becoming writers at all. This she accomplished by making many painful sacrifices. She was forced to adopt a defiant attitude toward those who held traditional opinions about women and their so-called roles, thus inviting much unneeded and undeserved criticism. She was forced to accept outrageously low wages for long hours of tedious work, during which time me she left her son in the care of others. She fought hard and long before she was taken seriously by the male artists and intellectuals of her day."

Spanish One: A beginning Spanish language textbook adopted by over 100 universities. Jones makes her textbook enjoyable by creating fictional university students who live in Madrid, and whose relationships develop as the chapters progress. Her talent as a creative writer makes this book a delight to teach. Strong emphasis on grammar. Published by Van Nostrand Reinhold, New York (two editions).

TO BE PUBLISHED IN APRIL, 2013

What is Love? (The Bible on Broadway)

The author taught this book several times in manuscript form in the Adult Sunday School program and home Bible studies at All Nations Christian Reformed Church in Halifax, Nova Scotia, and also for Intervarsity Student Fellowship. Starting with the fourteenth-century Troubadours and ending with comments by C.S. Lewis, it is a fresh new look at the Bible as it applies to three Broadway musicals: *The Phantom of the Opera, Man of La Mancha,* and *Les Misérables.*

Sonia (Harrison) Jones is listed in *Who's Who in the East, International Authors and Writers Who's Who, The World Who's Who of Women, and Who's Who in Canada*

ABOUT THE AUTHOR

Sonia Harrison Jones was born in England, educated in the U.S., and spent the rest of her life in Canada (it isn't over yet). After receiving her PhD from Harvard in Romance Languages and Literatures, she chaired the Department of Spanish at Dalhousie University in Halifax for many years.

She and her husband bought a cow in an unguarded moment, but Daisy's bountiful milk production was too much for their little family to handle. So they began a small yogurt business which eventually became a multi-million dollar enterprise. The corporation was so successful that the feds, of course, found a way to regulate it right out of existence.

Now Sonia is well into her third career, writing books a mile a minute. She has written ten books in various genres, and is looking forward to writing many more. For further information please go to www.erserandpond.com.

www.ingramcontent.com/pod-product-compliance
Lightning Source LLC
Chambersburg PA
CBHW050110280326
41933CB00010B/1039